DON ANTHONY (*above*) lectures on comparative aspects of sport and physical education at Avery Hill College, England. He is a pioneer in Britain of the study of comparative sport, particularly in Eastern Europe and the Third World, having written his Master's thesis on 'Comparative Physical Education' and obtained his doctorate on the 'Role of Physical Education and Sport in Developing Countries' (both at the University of Leicester). For several years he was a consultant to Unesco and the Council of Europe, and adviser on sport to the IAAF and to several commercial companies. More recently, he was co-founder of the Centre for International Sport Studies and initiator of the British International Festival of Sports Film and Television (Videosport). He is President of the English Volleyball Association, and initiated the formation of a national body for this sport in Great Britain.

A former British Olympic hammer-thrower, he is a well-known sportswriter and commentator, having worked for the BBC at both the Mexico and Montreal Olympics. Among his publications are *Know the Game*; *Keeping Fit for All Ages*; *Volleyball – Do It This Way*; and *The Dunlop P.E. Teacher's Handbook*. He is married to a graduate of the Warsaw Academy of Physical Culture, and they have one son, Marek.

A STRATEGY FOR BRITISH SPORT

DON ANTHONY

A STRATEGY FOR BRITISH SPORT

C. HURST & COMPANY
LONDON
McGILL-QUEEN'S UNIVERSITY PRESS
MONTREAL

First published in the United Kingdom
by C Hurst & Co (Publishers) Ltd.
1-2 Henrietta Street, London WC2 8PS

Published simultaneously in Canada
by McGill-Queen's University Press
1020 Pine Avenue West, Montreal H3A 1A2

ISBNs
U.K.: 0-905838-42-4
Canada: 0-7735-0531-8

Legal deposit second quarter 1980
Bibliothèque Nationale du Québec

To Jadwiga, Marek and George

*Typeset by Red Lion Setters
Holborn, London
and Printed in Great Britain
by Billing & Sons Ltd.
Guildford, London and Worcester*

PREFACE

Originally I intended this book to appear *after* the Moscow Olympic Games. It was to have concluded with a chapter evaluating them. The sudden debate on British sports administrative problems, launched in 1979 by the President of the Central Council of Physical Recreation, Prince Philip, in the *Guardian* and in public addresses, caused me to think again. The Minister for Sport and Recreation was forced to comment. The Sports Council took a stance. The British Olympic Association was concerned also, having set the organisation of the 1988 Olympic Games in London as a major target.

I want to thank several people for inspiration and guidance. First Philip Noel-Baker, world statesman and great man, for twenty years of fun and friendship in sport; every moment with him has been a joy and an education in living. I thank William Jones, life Secretary General of the International Amateur Basketball Federation, for a similar long term friendship; his worldly-wisdom has often made me reconsider my views and prejudices. I thank Bob Wight, Director of Physical Education at Leicester University, for his constant kindness and sincerity; his persistence and loyalty have enabled me and others to study at higher degree level in sport and physical education. We all owe him much. I thank Basil Stamatakis, for thirty-eight years lecturer at Loughborough University, for his unflagging friendship and inspiration; a true physical educationist whose personal example has been of great value to generations of students at Loughborough. Lastly I thank the many students who have passed through my hands during the last thirty years; I have learnt so much from them and they continue to make my life a delight. In a somewhat different context I thank my schnauzer-dog for getting me closer to nature again and teaching me the value of regular walks. Walking is the *basic* sport for all, and more propaganda could be devoted to it.

I did not think my manuscript was ready when I handed it to the publisher, and I do not think it is ready now, even after it has been through the editing process. But in a lifetime of sport I have learnt that one is *never* ready for competition. There is always that little more skill needed, that tiny touch of speed, another level of strength. The athlete must go to his blocks or step into the circle always, in his own opinion, unready. There must be that final step in the dark. This is my step in the dark.

Finally, I alone am responsible for the opinions expressed in this book. These opinions are not necessarily those of any of the organisations with which I am connected.

October 1979 DON ANTHONY

CONTENTS

1

INTRODUCTION

Unesco's consultative committee on sport and physical education has defined sport as follows: 'Any physical activity which has the character of play and which involves a struggle with oneself or with others, or a confrontation with natural elements, is a sport. If this activity involves competition it must then always be performed in a spirit of sportsmanship. There can be no true sport without the idea of fairplay. Sport, thus defined, is a remarkable means of education.'

The World Health Organisation (WHO), in its definition of health, calls for a complete state of physical, social and mental wellbeing.

In this book, when I talk about 'sport' I lean heavily on these twin roots—education and health. I don't wish to trip over definition at every stage and I don't intend to be pedantic in the matter. I am not a jargon-man. The activities involved range from the recreative to the highly competitive. They will also include those under the umbrella term 'physical education'. The definition of the terms *physical education* and *sport* have become a neurotic preoccupation for some. If we were German, 'sport' would probably suffice (note the German National College for sport and physical education—the Cologne *Sporthochschule*). For both the French and the Anglo-Saxons, definition in this area has become a stamping ground for philosophers and lovers of semantics.

'Physical education' has been defined as 'education through the physical and by the physical'. It is concerned with such objectives as the development of physique, the promotion of efficient body systems, and the development of physical skills in sport. Children are put into situations where they must solve physical questions in a physical way; where they experience enjoyment and challenge; where they relate to others in groups; and where they must exercise judgement on such matters as morality, competition, collaboration, leadership, followership and self-denial. It is hoped that exposure to this range of physical activities will help children understand, and become part of, traditional culture of local, national, regional and international proportions. Physical education can be 'playful', but it has an element of direction and purpose about it. 'Play' is something spontaneous, absorbing, self-contained and self-sufficient. Sport also contains 'play', but it is a regulated form of play which need not carry with it the *conscious* educational motives which characterise physical education.

Between play, sport and physical education there is overlap — and sometimes conflict. Where there is conflict, or the need to limit the range, or the need to categorise and put into an order of priorities — I turn to the principles of education and health, and those of civilised conduct between people and nations.

The most popular and charismatic expression of these principles — and the most astonishing combination of sport, physical education and play — is the modern Olympic movement. Its Founder, Baron Pierre de Coubertin (1863-1937), was philosopher, statesman, sportsman, educationist, physical educationist and visionary. For all its faults the Olympic movement is still the most powerful source of inspiration for sport — and for sportsmen and sportswomen. One reason why I write this book with renewed hope for British sport is the possibility that in 1988 the Olympic Games may return to London, where they were also held in 1908 and 1948. The 1988 Games would be exactly right for us at this moment; we would have to put our house in order administratively and philosophically. We would *have* to get our methods and principles right; we would have to face and solve problems which we currently tend to obscure, deny or dodge. Our sports administrators would have to be dragged into the twenty-first century. We would have to 'think British' for a change. For too long we have been able to have four bites at the World Cup — England, Scotland, Wales, Northern Ireland — a fact which irritates federated states: in the Olympic movement we are recognised as Great Britain, and we should start to think that way more often. We would be forced to think out clearly the relationships between 'amateur' and 'professional' sport; we would need to devise efficient and ethical means of selecting and training talent, and we would have to structure a system which recognised our social responsibilities towards the champion — and the champion's responsibility towards society. Because we, as hosts, would have automatic right of entry to all the Olympic sport competitions, our plan of attack would need to be perfectly balanced. There would be an end to falling back on our soccer heritage and sending the rest of the sporting family to the wall; handball, volleyball, wrestling, as well as athletics and swimming, would all get a fair crack of the whip. We would also have a chance to organise a Games which might 'humanise' the Olympic movement, and balance — but not eliminate — the 'technological' emphasis which has almost become self-defeating.

Human problems have been another spur to the writing of this book. When one's own children become involved in 'the system', everything becomes clearer. A theoretician like myself has to stand up and be counted. My son attends an excellent comprehensive school. I have no complaints about the facilities or the staff. But I do query the *actuality* of his situation — an actuality which means that, at the crucial development age of fourteen, his physical education and sport programme, in the curriculum, boil down to one visit a week to the local sports centre. This visit involves a short swim and a game of badminton. As far as I can understand, that is everything — for the week. At no time during the week is there anyone pointing out postural problems while moving and sitting; there is no one dealing with breathing. In a sense his body has been abandoned. There is no one conscientiously concerned, primarily, with emotional and sensory education through physical activity; 'education' has become synonymous with 'intellectual education'. Outside the curriculum programme, there is the opportunity for representative games playing for the school, but solely for the high achiever. Not enough is provided in our schools for the child of middle ability who would appreciate — not striving for the ultimate, but a directed programme requiring discipline, regularity and effort. People like myself who train teachers must accept some of the blame for this. There must be many parents in the country aware of this situation.

The same problem exists among the clubs. Most sports clubs look for a fairly high degree of skill before accepting new members. Many, it is true, have junior membership schemes but there are too few clubs. It came as a shock to me to find out in 1978 that there was no gymnastic club for children near to Holland Park — nothing in central London as far as I could determine at the time. If you live in central London and your child is good at gymnastics, be prepared to make long journeys to Lewisham or Harrow!

It is not that the facilities are poor. I know of few countries that can match our provision of school gymnasia and sports halls, our abundance of parks, soccer pitches, tennis courts and swimming pools. I have worked for twenty years at a luxurious College of Education in South East London. On two of its sides, the site of the College is flanked by acres of excellent sports facilities of all kinds and for all ages; ten fine grass tennis courts are nearest. Lining the other sides are enormous housing estates. But there is little or no contact between the College and the people who live in the housing estates. The seven all-weather tennis courts and the all-weather hockey area are never used for vacation courses, nor are the three gymnasia. The industrial organisations that own the sports grounds use them no more than twice a week — for pitifully few people.

Again there is no *local* involvement. For twenty years successive ministers have made noises about this, but there has been no substantial change.

Of course we cannot *abandon* these facilities to local youth groups, the housewives, the elderly, the handicapped and others for free-play. The factor which could marry the people to the places is a profession of community sport and recreation workers. We have the chance today to establish a new sports coaching and recreational service — a service which will bring these under-used facilities to life.

As a professional sports teacher for thirty years I have become horrified at the intrusion of commerce — unthinking commerce — into sport. I see sport as a humanistic exercise connected with education in its widest sense and with health for the community. I see it as fun and the provider of adventure and challenge. I do not see it as the plaything of commerce, or as a billboard for any product. I want sportsmen to be thinking people and to make choices. I resent their being exploited in sales campaigns for products at best irrelevant and at worst dangerous. This is not to say that I am opposed to all sponsorship and patronage for sport. But I am totally opposed to the growing tendency to *surrender leadership* of the sports movement to commerce. Leadership should be retained by teachers, those who know that the cradle of the whole sports movement is the schools sports movement. It is mainly as a teacher, therefore, that I speak.

As a teacher of physical education students I am opposed to those who would make sport and physical education enormously complicated and extremely boring. The human body has been the same in its structure and needs for several million years and is likely to remain so — a fact which those who work in the professions connected with the body should contemplate with humility. There is absolutely no need to complicate the study and practice of sport. With the search for academic status, physical education and sports studies have been invaded by philosophers, psychologists, sociologists, ethologists (character and sport), ethnologists (race and sport), anthropologists, cultural scientists, kinesiologists, aestheticians, and others. They have every right to use sport as a research field for the illumination of their own problems, but this should not be confused with the straightforward study of sport. Sports studies should be concerned with the front-line problems of a non-lingual world phenomenon — a social movement involving hundreds of millions of people who get great pleasure from the skills and struggles of sports. Sports studies, like sport itself, should take place in an atmosphere of fun and enthusiasm —

which does not at all mean that such studies cannot also be serious.

Many of these problems arise from the fact that sport in Britain 'just developed'. We have never been quite sure whether sport consists of 'playing about' or 'war without weapons'. It is not right to place international sport in the hands of a self-electing group of mainly white and mainly rich persons; nor is it right to place it in the hands of international civil servants who will give it the bureaucratic treatment and no heart. Sport is about heart — about devotion, and love, and passion. Not only among those who practice sport, but equally those — in their hundreds of thousands — who coach, officiate and administer, mostly for no financial gain. But *gain* they do. Frustrated businessmen find self-expression and satisfaction on the boards of soccer clubs; director and caretaker can experience role-reversal in a team game; young and old can find that sports groups might replace the extended family.

Pick up a newspaper anywhere in the world and you can find two or three pages devoted entirely to sport. Study the television and radio services anywhere and there will be a similar emphasis. After food and sex (usually in that order), man's greatest appetite is for sport. Because of its non-lingual nature, sport is a medium for easy communication between peoples. Because of its physical nature it seems to satisfy an innate need for muscular expression in mankind. The world sports movement has a code of ethics (fairplay) and a rule of law; it has a mass appeal of incomparable power.

Despite all this, world sport is a mere infant. In its modern forms it is less than a century old. The first international sports federation, for gymnastics, was established only in 1881, and those for skating and rowing followed eleven years later. The first International Olympic Committee was constituted in 1894. The ancient Olympic movement lasted for more than 1,000 years, so that compared to it the modern sports movement is an immature child. Is it surprising that it lacks a clear sense of identity, appears to lose its sense of direction, and sometimes makes mistakes?

Politicians respect its power and occasionally abuse its principles. It has been used by women in the quest for emancipation. Its situations of contrived conflict, in competitive games, are civilised by quaint ceremonies and rituals. Its varied forms enable the generations to meet in friendly exercise or rivalry. It is commonly accepted as part of a truly balanced education.

World sport is an integral part of world culture; its forms can serve to develop aesthetic taste and can satisfy the need for artistic expression. It has its own history, its own science, its own cultural reservoir. Its devotees are concerned with the search for excellence; they reach out to the limits of athletic endeavour and they try to create new and yet newer patterns of movement. They practise in their millions; they observe in their hundreds of millions. The stadium can be the theatre of the masses; it can be a shrine for the glory of sport; it can be a laboratory for the study of effort; a patron of architecture and fine arts; a forum for audience participation and for group therapy; a health centre, a community club, a public park. It can also be a piece of real estate, with no social role, used only for profit-making once or twice a week.

The sportsman can wallow in the joy of sensuous muscular effort. Through sports participation he can appreciate beauty and he can sometimes create it. He can stimulate his senses by finely executed skills and by passionate competitive dramas. He can come to know what it means to be a delicately tuned human animal. He can also be corrupted by sport; he may never learn to win and lose gracefully; he may be so stricken with big-headedness that he can never re-adjust to everyday life when his playing days are over.

It seems to me that most of the more recent studies on sports have been observations by outsiders, looking in. This exercise is useful and valid, but too often it does not go far enough. Those on the inside — addicts to the drug of sport, who feel that man is programmed to play at sport whether or not he can find a reason — are thus challenged to something more than just 'doing'. They must reflect and publish. I love sport; I have devoted my life to the practice, teaching and study of sport. In this pursuit I have travelled the world for thirty years. I therefore want to look at world sport from the *inside*, outwards.

It is more and more my feeling that sport is just as much real life as much of what passes for work. Certainly, in many sports it is possible to experience a wholeness, a taste of wholesome creative physical and mental effort, which one does not find in one's daily labour. On the other hand, sport is not more important than life itself. The man is always more important than the athlete; human happiness and understanding are more important than sporting success. For example, there is a certain nobility about great athletes who make their stand against racial discrimination more important than the possible winning of a gold medal in the Olympics. We should not forget that young people have often made the supreme sacrifice for such principles.

As we near the end of a century of organised international sport it is time to take stock, and to ask questions about the origins of sport, about its original objectives and about its present state. Because I feel that sport is an enriching experience, I want to share that feeling with others. In many ways — apart from that emotional conviction — I am at the beginning of a journey in uncharted country and I ask the reader to explore it with me.

My exploration must, however, be one with limited objectives. I cannot cover every problem. I concentrate on British sports problems since these are close to me; but I see them and my analysis of them only as an example. Aspects of the British pattern can be found elsewhere and some of my criticism about specific situations in Britain might be of use generally in the world of sport. This will be a committed, prescriptive book. It will assemble impressions, generalisations, approximations. I have tried to be a catalyst.

I started my manuscript on a day when a footballer changed clubs for £1 million, and at a time when a punter can win £800,000 on the 'Pools' but whole communities are at the same time denied the basic facilities and coaching to enjoy sport. I inherited a love of sport from my teachers, from my friends and from my fellow-competitors. International competitive sport has enriched my life. When I hear modern prima donnas of the sports arenas complaining about their lot, I groan. Sport has given to most of them a sense of identity, a sense of commitment and a means of expression. They should go down on their knees and thank sport for what it has done for them. It owes them nothing. They owe *it* a lifetime's devotion.

This book is for the general reader, to describe something of the world of sport. It is also for the people who are actively involved in teaching, coaching, and organising sport. It might also be of use to teachers in secondary schools who are looking for 'project studies' in the humanities. Many of the questions raised in this text can be researched by young people at school, especially looking at their local situation: the relationship of sport to music and other fine arts, the origin of local games, hobbies connected with sports, law and sport, ethical and moral questions, intelligent sports televiewing — a whole host of questions in which sport is part of social studies.

2

HOW SPORT IS ORGANISED IN BRITAIN

In an area of free choice like sport, there is little point in looking for complete administrative tidiness. Wherever one looks in the world there is a similar problem — how can a country relate its sports administrative systems to the governmental system in general and how can the state sector and the private sector, in sport administration, relate to each other? At ministerial level there are many differences. In Poland sport and tourism were linked; in Sweden sport and agriculture; in Egypt sport and youth. In some countries the link is made with defence, entertainment or health. In many, education is selected as the peg. In East Germany we find a 'State Committee for Physical Culture', its President having access to the cabinet. We could find an increase, in the future, of high-ranking Ministers for Sport and Leisure as the silicon chip age really dawns.

The British situation is unique. It is a mixture of tradition, compromise, 'Euro-imitation' and bloody-mindedness. The Minister of State for Sport and Recreation works within the Department of the Environment. A civil servant within this Ministry is appointed to brief the Minister and has a team of other civil servants to assist him. Other Ministries have an interest and must be accommodated in policy statements: e.g. Health, Education and those responsible for water, forests and land-use. There are occasions where other sectors of government are directly involved, as with violence on the terraces: an obvious concern of the Home Office. The Minister appoints the Chairman of the Sports Council and the members of this Council. We have seen recently how a Minister can reject the first choice of the Sports Council for the post of Director, and 'impose' another candidate. Since both the 'Ministry' and the 'Council' are still 'young', in governmental terms, such a situation is understandable, but it must not be perpetuated.

The Sports Section of the Department of the Environment has a staff of approximately fifty persons, dealing with such matters as sports policy, liaison with the Sports Council, development of sport, football crowd behaviour, sponsorship, international aspects of sport, apartheid, Council of Europe meetings, social aspects of sport, medicine and doping, and sport facilities for the disabled and for inner cities. Additionally the Minister takes advice from expert 'working parties' which are set up from time to time; one on centres of excellence reported in 1978. It is also within the Minister's power to appoint paid advisers; Sir Walter Winterbottom was thus appointed in 1978 to advise on international affairs. It is thought that the Conservative Government elected in 1979 will shift more direct executive power from the Department of the Environment team to the Sports Council. Founded as an advisory body in 1965, the Council was created, as an executive body, by Royal Charter in 1972. An attempt is made to balance the Council's membership so that all sporting interests are represented, but the members are asked to concern themselves with 'sport in general' rather than their special sports interests. In its own report for 1976/7 the Sports Council stated that it 'values its independence in deciding its policies and stating its views on the promotion of sport'. In addition to the members there are a Chairman and two Vice-Chairmen, all these posts being part-time and paid. Furthermore, one finds a Director and Administrator and a hierarchy of officers from Principal Executive Officer downwards. This hierarchy is not only London-based. The Sports Council has more than 600 officers, whose salaries are determined by the Civil Service, and employees structured on a regional basis as follows: Northern; North-West; Yorkshire and Humberside; East Midlands; West Midlands; Eastern; Greater London and South-East; Southern; South-West. The Council also administers the national sports centres at the Crystal Palace, Bisham Abbey, Lilleshall Hall, Plas y Brenin (mountain activities), the National Sailing Centre at Cowes, and the Holme Pierrepoint National Water Sports Centre in Nottingham. The Council is attended by observers from the Sports Council for Northern Ireland, the Scottish Sports Council, the Sports Council for Wales, the Department of the Environment, the Department of Education and Science, and the Central Council of Physical Recreation (CCPR). At district and town level there is also a growth of voluntary 'sport councils'.

The Council 'has the responsibility to allocate funds for the development of sport and physical recreation'. Its policy is shaped and kept under review by members serving on specialised committees, and 'continuous background work is done by staff of the liaison, promotion, facilities and research teams — both at headquarters and in the regions'. The Council has specialised committees in sports development, information and research, facilities, finance and general purposes. It negotiates with local Authorities on the question of constructing community sports facilities.

A United Kingdom Affairs Committee brings together the Sports

Councils for England, Wales, Scotland and Northern Ireland. The structure of the Sports Council for Wales is a case in point. The basic organisational model is the same as for England, with specialised committees for development and for facilities, and one for the National Sports Centre. An integral part of the Council, however, is the Welsh Sports and Games Association. Fifty-seven sports governing bodies in Wales are in membership of this Association.

The Scottish Sports Council received its Royal Charter in 1972, and the previously existing Scottish Council of Physical Recreation was wound up. The Royal Charter included a requirement that the new Council would create a forum through which governing bodies could make their views known. This is called the Standing Conference on Sport: its Chairman is appointed by the Secretary of State for Scotland and serves on the Scottish Sports Council, which provides the secretariat. The situation left much to be desired, and in 1978 an 'Association of Governing Bodies of Sport' was formed in Scotland, which now includes 30 out of the 66 governing bodies which form the Standing Conference. A statement gave the reasons for the formation of this new body: there was a need for a collective voice for Scottish sport, and there was dissatisfaction with the way sport was supported and promoted in Scotland. Scottish sports bodies, the statement continued, wanted to build a close relationship with local authorities regarding local sports provision; the local authorities and the governing bodies of the major sports were felt to be the 'two key groups' involved in sporting opportunities for large numbers of ordinary youngsters and adults. More revenue for Scottish sport was needed, to be 'brought under democratic control'. There was need for a forum for discussion; such topics as organisation of major international events, sponsorship, relations with local education authorities, minisports, etc., were worthy of treatment by seminars. There was need also for a solution to the critical financial questions: securing grant aid from the Sports Council; profiting from a commercial lottery; making a special relationship for all sports governing bodies with one travel operator, and thus securing cheap transportation rates. This Association was born out of frustration with the arrangement whereby the sports bodies are represented in the Scottish Sports Council as a 'committee'. Critics of this arrangement feel that the Chairman of the sports committee should have been elected and not appointed; also that the members of the Sports Council are not accountable, and its policies are inconsistent and lack clear direction. They say that the Scottish Sports Council spends too much money on its internal administration (a point also made by critics of the Sports Council in England); that it duplicates the work of regional and district local authorities; that it does not secure adequate funding for Scottish sport from the United Kingdom budget; and that it is not making much impact on the development of sport and recreation in Scotland.

In England too there is a problem. The sports governing bodies collectively have not yet found a contented role *vis-à-vis* the Sports Council. The Central Council of Physical Recreation (CCPR) proclaims itself 'the independent voice of sport and recreation'. Some 200 voluntary sports organisations are in membership of the CCPR, and from their delegates to it are elected an Executive Committee and specialised committees for: water recreation, outdoor pursuits, major spectator sports, games and sports, movement and dance, and the 'division of interested organisations'. Already it is clear that an overlap exists and that there are possible areas of conflict regarding the committee work of the Sports Council (England) and the CCPR. In its Annual Report for 1976/7 the Executive Committee of the CCPR made a statement on its relationship with the Sports Council. An attempt to solve the problem has been the facility granted to the CCPR to nominate seven members of the Sports Council. However, the Executive states:

> The Memorandum of the CCPR and the Royal Charter of the Sports Council refer to the special role of the CCPR as a consultative body to the Sports Council. Though the CCPR nominees are free to exercise their own judgements on Sports Council matters, it is of obvious importance that the CCPR views and opinions on matters of interest to Governing Bodies of sport and recreation should be made known to them. Arrangements should therefore be made for the CCPR nominees to meet from time to time, and the General Secretary of the CCPR as an observer on the Sports Council should ensure that matters of CCPR interest, which appear on Sports Council agenda, are brought to the attention of the CCPR nominees, and that the General Secretary should report to the Executive Committee on such matters as he has raised. However, the CCPR should play its full part as a consultative body and should take all steps possible, in liaison with the Sports Council, to ensure that the contribution the CCPR can make to the work of the Sports Council is fully realised. To that end in order to make the special relationship between the CCPR and the Sports Council meaningful, then the views of the CCPR upon specific projects should be sought by the Sports Council at a much earlier stage than has occurred in the past.

Unfortunately this expressed good grace has not worked in practice. Over the involvement of tobacco companies in sport sponsorship, the CCPR caucus of nominees to the Sports Council used its 'block vote' in 1978 to embarrass the Sports Council and particularly the newly-appointed Chairman. Publicity stunts involving delegations to prominent persons and places are made separately more than collectively by the two organisations. In 1979, a complaint on the question of funds left over in the Sports Council's account for 1978/9, was made by representatives of the CCPR directly to the Prime Minister. All this is made more incomprehensible when it is realised that the two organisations share the same building, and that, broadly, salaries for officers come from the same purse.

Although the CCPR can be blamed for clumsiness and one-upmanship, the Sports Council is no innocent. In particular it has behaved in an unthinking way over matters of Olympic policy. In 1977 it published a major policy statement on the 'Open Olympics' without consulting the British Olympic Association. The statement suggests that the categories 'amateur' and 'professional' be abolished in favour of 'players', the matter of being paid taking second place to fairplay and sportsmanship. Although it has every right to act independently, common courtesy, if not protocol, suggests that there should be collaboration. The 'protocol' argument arose again in 1979 when an invitation arrived from Moscow for the Minister for Sport and Recreation regarding the Spartakiade of 1979. This event, held periodically during the last fifty years, has been internationalised for the first time, with the main purpose of giving the organisers of the 1980 Olympic Games in Moscow a training run, and the participating countries a chance to gain experience prior to the Games. Since there is no such thing as 'officially recognised pre-Olympic events', protocol in this matter is, it is true, a little blurred. Although there could be some confusion about who is responsible for multisport events in Britain, it is blatantly clear that it is *not* the Sports Council. The invitation was passed by the Minister to the Sports Council and there, regrettably, it stayed. The body which should obviously have been consulted was of course the British Olympic Association, which is the national Olympic committee. The BOA will have the responsibility for organising the British team for Moscow in 1980 and needs every opportunity possible in the areas of team organisation and logistics. A chance for wholehearted collaboration round a specific front-line project — by *all* concerned — was muddled and muddied.

It could of course be said that the British Olympic Association brought this on its own head — historically. Had the BOA seen its traditional brief as wider than fund-raising, and more to be a fully-fledged multisports body, affiliating not only the twenty-six Olympic sports but also, as associates, all other sports bodies and interested parties — as is the case in many other countries including Italy and France — there would have been no need for the existence of the CCPR or the Sports Council. It must be said nevertheless that traditionally the BOA was a very successful fund-raiser; few British sportspeople failed to reach the Olympics due to lack of finance. Indeed it could be said that the development of other initiatives like the Sports Aid Foundation, the nefarious CCPR association with the tobacco company State Express, the International Athletes Club 'Moscow Olly' campaign, and 'British Action for Solidarity in Sport', have served to detract from the powerful and charismatic 'Olympic appeal'. With too many groups climbing on the appeals wagon there has been confusion and even doubt among those who might gladly give.

The old British Olympic Association concentrated almost entirely on fund-raising; it can be said fairly that it neglected its duty to promote actively an ongoing Olympic education programme. Since 1978, however, there has been a striking reform in both its constitution and its programme. The current British Olympic Association is composed of elected members from the twenty-six Olympic sports; the two members of the International Olympic Committee in Britain, Lord Luke and the Marquis of Exeter; a Chairman, Sir Denis Follows; and two professional officers at General Secretary and Deputy General Secretary level, with a supporting secretarial staff of some eight persons. Its specialised committees concern medicine, education, membership and 'Olympic Day'. It is *British* in conception and is the one sports body which can offer both institutional and individual membership. Its Appeals Organiser has the responsibility to raise money for British participation in the Games — the Olympics and the Winter Olympics. As anyone who has ever organised a sports club, or any club, knows — it is not the amount of money raised which matters in the end, but the solidarity which *trying* to raise money builds. The BOA's function as a national Olympic committee is clear; it also has a broad-based 'Council' which involves other sports bodies with an interest in Olympism; and it partly provides a home and support for the Commonwealth Games committees. The newly-instituted 'Olympic Day', bringing the BOA into line with most other national Olympic committees which even organise 'national games', could augur well for the future. A multi-sport occasion held annually could be a foundation stone for administrative accord rather than rivalry.

The membership of these three bodies, the Sports Council, the Central Council for Physical Recreation and the British Olympic Association (National Olympic Committee) reveals a slender thread of cohesion through the multiple membership of some individuals. Mary Glen-Haig is Chairman of the CCPR, a member of the Sports Council and a member of the National Olympic Committee as delegate from the sport of fencing which says something for the emancipation of women in British sport. Others cover two organisations. Among these are Sir Denis Follows who is Chairman of the British Olympic Association and Treasurer of the CCPR; W. Holland, who sits on the National Olympic Committee for weight-lifting and is an Executive Committee member of the CCPR; C. Palmer, who is also President of the World Judo Federation and Secretary General of the Assembly of International Sport Federations, sits on the Executive of the CCPR and is Vice-Chairman of the British Olympic Association; K. Mitchell is both a Sports Council member and Executive member of the CCPR. Such multi-membership is more accidental than planned, however, and a situation *could* arise where three organisations would be overlapping continuously with no consultation at any level.

It would be untrue to suggest that this triad truly represents British sport in terms of 'opinion'; the separate national governing bodies for sport are, individually, closer to the grass roots and sometimes extremely jealous of their autonomy. In many senses, after all, the different national governing bodies are rival customers for the same product: the schools physical education system sends out — we hope — children highly motivated towards permanent sports participation: the sports governing bodies then vie with each other to attract recruits. The bigger bodies like the Football Association, the Rugby Union and the MCC are not noted for collaborative consultation and action. In many countries the larger and richer sports bodies 'mother' the smaller and poorer ones. The soccer section of Real Madrid, for example, is well-known in Britain, but on the continent Real Madrid's basketball team and its representative teams in other sports are just as well known. In Britain 'insularity' is almost of disease proportions. Such single-mindedness can cause grave problems internationally. In 1979, the International Olympic Committee warned the French Rugby Union that the planned tour by the white South African 'Springbok' rugby team could result in the French team being banned from the 1980 Olympic Games. In France such a threat carries muscle since the French Rugby Union is in membership with the French National Olympic Committee. In Britain a threat to the Rugby Union might be treated lightly by the rugby administrators, who have not in the past demonstrated much vision or understanding on matters concerning the 'unity of sports', and the ethical basis of international sports competition.

Some might say that many people in rugby care not a jot for the success of the Olympic movement — perhaps displaying the same selfish and careless disregard for the sports movement in general as did their counterparts in New Zealand before the 1976 Games. The result on that occasion was the withdrawal of the black African nations from the Games, and the bitter disappointment of their competitors. A similar threat to the Moscow Games would be presented if further South African rugby tours took place. At the time of writing, the latest team to be invited is named 'the Quaggas', which apologists falsely liken to 'the Barbarians'. It is composed of eight Blacks, eight Whites and eight Coloureds, a structure blatantly reinforcing the principles of apartheid, and betraying the cardinal principle of selection on merit. The French and Irish governments banned this tour. The British government did not.

Should it surprise us that rugby is the worst culprit in this matter? The Rugby Union conducting a spiteful vendetta against Rugby League for many years, the 'Home Unions' not playing with the many more countries affiliated to the International Amateur Rugby Union. The puzzling resistance to leagues based on ability in favour of a difficult-to-understand 'old boy' arrangement of fixtures leads to a system of team selection at national level which must leave room for doubt. Just how does a lowly rugby team fight its way to the top of the pile? Discriminatory attitudes seem inbuilt.

There is no compulsion on individual sports bodies to join the CCPR since this is a free assembly, but most, if not all, sports organisations are in membership. Certainly the twenty-six Olympic sports—i.e. those sports at present accepted for the Olympic programme—are represented on the National Olympic Committee (British Olympic Association). The Sports Council reaches most sectors through its grant-giving activities. Public money now reaches voluntary sports organisations, both individual and collective. Grants for administration are, in this way, available for the CCPR, the British Olympic Association, the many separate sports governing bodies, approved research projects, and the internal administration of the Sports Council itself—the last-named, incidentally, receiving a considerable sum. Unfortunately, from time to time the Sports Council appears to forget that it is an agency fairly distributing *public* money—not an organisation handing out its own money!

The aims of the national sports governing bodies are, in short, to encourage the development of the sport; to ensure the proper conduct of the sport; to select national representative teams, and to represent the country on the appropriate international federation. The structure starts at grass roots level with clubs, which form district, country and regional associations on a geographical basis, and these run their own courses for coaches, referees and other officials. There is a growing interest in what is for Britain the new development of 'Centres of Excellence'; these can work only if the Sports Councils and national sports bodies collaborate with real enthusiasm. National governing bodies are controlled by elected honorary officers with, in most cases, a back-up service of paid administrators. The Sports Council facilitate this. Four hundred officials of this kind have up to 75 per cent of their salaries funded in this way.

There is a further category of sports organisations which could be called 'educational'. This includes bodies with special roles in sport like universities, colleges and polytechnics. I mention these separately since even here there seems to be interminable disunity. Not only are there separate bodies for the three types of higher education but there are also separate organisations for men and for women. An attempt to weld the student sports movement into a cohesive whole exists in the shape of the British Students' Sports Federation, but this is powerful only in respect of Britain's involvement in international events like the World Student Games. At school level the picture is better, with schools associations for most individual sports and a growing corporate body called the National Council for Schools Sports. Here again the national schools body relates to the international world of school sport. Much of this activity is hidden from the public by an unimaginative — and irresponsible — sports press. An example of this is the annual schools athletics championships which draw crowds of some 15,000 and are a model of organisational skill and participant enthusiasm. Rarely does this magnificent event reach the newspapers or the visual media; if it does, it receives only a passing mention. The problems — basic to every family in the country — of schools physical education scarcely ever find their way into the columns of national newspapers.

Finally there are those many special interest organisations which are important in policy planning for sport. They include the National Playing Fields Association, the British Sports Writers Association, the British Association for National Coaches, and bodies representing the handicapped, sports medicine and local government recreation officers.

Private sports clubs are also a powerful group in Britain, but they are not 'organised' collectively in any true sense. A large number of sports grounds throughout the country are owned by industrial enterprises; these are often some way from the work place and, although often of excellent design and kept in fine condition, they are used by relatively few people; many receive support from 'associate' members who live near the facility but do not work at the enterprise. Tennis and bowls clubs are another traditional group; these might also offer squash and indoor sports like billiards and darts. Many of these exist because of the drinking members! Profits from the bar and the gambling machines keep the active-sports fees down. Hockey and cricket clubs might combine. Athletics clubs usually plough a lonely furrow; as do soccer and rugger clubs. Golf clubs are also mainly private institutions, although local authorities have moved into this area more forcefully in the last decade. An example of such enterprise is at Dartford, Kent, where the local authority funds a superb golf course at Lullingstone Park; an 18-hole and a 9-hole course are provided, and there is an excellent clubhouse. Many of these private clubs have excellent social sides to their corporate life; members organise discos, dinners and car rallies; they also voluntarily water the courts by rota, and paint, repair and generally service the facilities, in addition to paying an annual fee. In recent years the growth of 'health clubs' has accelerated; these are commercial enterprises based on exercise machines, saunas and plush surroundings.

Professional soccer clubs, being private commercial enterprises, fall outside the mainstream of national sports organisation. There are only muted cries to bring them into the national pattern of sport. The majority of professional clubs are, however, affiliated to their own governing body, the Football League. The League organises matches and leagues and now promotes its own cup competition. In short, this means that the main stadium in any British community is usually the soccer club; this can be found in the heart of an industrial community, and it is used not more than twice a week by twenty-two professional footballers. Its role in the community is minimal. It is owned and managed by a private board of directors as a commercial enterprise. Although in recent years a few clubs have improved their facilities, made changes and endeavoured to become more 'multi-sport' (Sunderland F.C., for example), these are only cosmetic, and my description is still basically true. It is astonishing that we tolerate it, and inexcusable that the Sports Council and CCPR do not use their collective powers to question, stridently, a 'system' which allows such waste of resources in sport.

The 'transfers' of these professional players involve payment of bigger sums in total than the annual Sports Council grant of £14 million. A single player can be bought and sold for more than £1 million. A strange tax regulation prevents money being ploughed back which could be spent on plant, creating more facilities, establishing exercise sections for mothers and infants, for the aged and the handicapped, for sports medicine, for sports research, and for employing coaches. All in all, we have a system of full-time professionals, in many cases playing no better than their part-time counterparts in other European countries (Malmö F.C. of Sweden, who reached the final of the European Cup against Nottingham Forest, are a team of part-timers) and, from the point of view of community development, an irresponsible outgrowth from the main mass sports movement.

This professional sports movement runs parallel to the mass sports movement. Betting on these matches generates, as we can find out weekly in press announcements, sums of money annually *many times* greater than the grant for the Sports Council. Large profits are earned by the Pools Promoters' Association but, much more important, a vast sum is paid out weekly to punters, single payments reaching £800,000 and more; even half of this would revolutionise the cash-flow of hard-pressed amateur sports organisations. The stimulation of individual greed, as against community need, has brought misery to many winners, and despair to those who care for communal development.

Finally I turn to the organisation of physical education. This presents a picture which is no tidier. If there is a national policy, it is represented by the Inspectorate at the Department of Education and Science. A number of Inspectors, led by a Staff Inspector, have special responsibilities for physical education in addition to some general duties. Inspectors cannot impose their views on the curriculum; they can only advise. Together with local Advisers (Organisers) for Physical Education, employed by local authorities, they can ensure that minimum teaching standards are upheld and can refuse to validate young teachers engaged on their probationary year (the first year of teaching in a state school is always on probation). The advisers usually have far too many schools to visit; a school is lucky if it gets one visit a year. Their alternative is to organise in-service courses at primary and secondary level; at these courses they can update the knowledge and ability of the teachers in the service of their authority. Other courses for which teachers may receive grant-aid from their authorities are organised by various professional associations and by colleges which tend to specialise in physical education. Among these associations are the biggest, the Physical Education Association of Great Britain and Northern Ireland; the British Association of Advisers in Physical Education; the physical education section of the National Association of Teachers in Further and Higher Education; the British Universities Physical Education Association; the North-West Counties Physical Education Association, the Scottish Physical Education Association, and several others. There is also the Physical Education Committee of the Schools Council which concerns itself with curriculum matters.

There are no longer *standard* textbooks at either primary or secondary level for teachers of physical education. At primary level, physical education is mainly handled by class teachers, although there are often special responsibility posts; this is more common when a man is appointed to oversee 'games' in a mixed primary school. In secondary schools, specialist teachers of physical education run the physical education departments. There is a substantial involvement of non-specialist teachers in the games programme, however, especially in the programme for boys. Out-of-school activities are still a feature of the physical education programmes of British schools, and with the growth of recreational programmes there has been a noticeable 'integration' of staff interests; for example, the craft teachers collaborate to design and construct canoes and sailing boats for use by the physical education department. The absence of a core programme common to the nation has resulted in unnecessary waste; it is not unknown for a teacher interested in fencing to order complete sets of equipment and clothing for, say, forty children. This teacher would depart after staying two years, to be replaced by one for whom judo has an appeal; he would add judo equipment to the store and depart after two years being replaced by one keen on canoeing, and so on. Teachers receive their education at many different colleges of education (or what were such colleges and are now independent colleges, parts of polytechnics, or absorbed into universities). A college or university is able to design its own courses of study; the amount of time devoted to the subjects studied varies from place to place.

In physical education, it has become impossible to explain exactly what is going on in the country at a given moment. Currently the Council for National Academic Awards and the Department of Education and Science, with the support of other bodies, are endeavouring to tie all the ends together and publish a directory of courses. One problem is terminology: 'physical training' changed to 'physical education', which in turn was intellectualised into 'basic movement', 'movement training', 'movement studies', 'art of movement' and 'art and science of movement'. The usual umbrella term for physical education, dance or a combination of these is today 'movement studies' or 'human movement studies'. Strangely, the end-result is rather what it always was: physical education teachers teaching the basics of several sports in the schools and having a stab at some form of gymnastics. The advisers can advise and the inspectors inspect, but the curriculum is still largely determined by the personal interests of, respectively, the head teacher and the head of the physical education department. Certainly the range of subjects is much wider. A child can expect to become acquainted with table tennis, skating, judo and badminton, in addition to the more normal exposure to the major games. Schools are bigger and there is often more chance to specialise in a sport of special interest; schools also make good use of nearby squash courts, swimming pools and sports centres. But I am not sure that the depth of knowledge in physical education teaching or the sense of commitment is greater than it was thirty years ago, or even as great. An attempt to create one umbrella body for the physical education profession started with the formation of the British Council for Physical Education some years ago. This body has never really been a success owing to internal strife and non-collaboration. A number of professional journals are published by several of the organisations I have mentioned, but there is not one authoritative yearbook which summarises opinion and knowledge for the young teacher. One such publication would do much to improve access to knowledge in this field. Is it too much to ask the several bodies to contribute a definitive summary of developments in their 'section' to a common yearbook? Research is limited to higher degree studies and the mostly private efforts of pitifully few lecturers. Access to foreign studies can be obtained by the fanatical and passionate, but these are not freely translated and generously published.

Until the last decade the 'organiser' of physical education for a local education authority would oversee the whole area of community recreation in a general way, but in recent years a new area of recreation management has developed. Local authorities have invested heavily in plant, and community sports halls have mushroomed. Some are used by schools and the community jointly; some are parts of school sites. They have managers and instructors. 'Advisers' on recreation are appointed by local authorities. In some cases the 'physical recreation' element is treated separately — in others it is lumped together with libraries, theatres, and other pursuits (sometimes even with cemeteries!). These local government recreation specialists are another 'group' — even if rather loosely organised at the moment — from which pressure can come.

To summarise this administrative pattern, we find the following main categories of interest:

The Minister for Sport and Recreation, supported by the interest of other government sectors such as health and education, with a permanent office of appointed civil servants, and memoranda prepared by advisers and expert 'working parties' established by the Minister. It is the Minister's responsibility to extract all he can from the Exchequer for spending on sport.

The Sports Council, an appointed body expressing independence of action, occasionally showing an ambivalent attitude to the Minister but, it seems, subject ultimately to the finality of his decisions. The Sports Council (for England) has to relate to separate Sports Councils for Scotland, Wales and Northern Ireland, and to its own regional sports councils. It is the responsibility of the Sports Council to distribute the grant from the Exchequer fairly and wisely throughout the world of sport. All its members are appointed, not elected.

The Central Council of Physical Recreation, which is both a consultative body to the Sports Council and a freestanding organisation representing a wide spectrum of sports bodies, youth organisations, keep fit associations, and organisations with even a fringe interest in recreation. The CCPR has the right to nominate a number of members to the Sports Council. Its own committees are elected from delegates (themselves elected) from the separate member-bodies. It is served by a small number of professional officers; their salaries and the rent for its accommodation (it shares the same building as the Sports Council) are met mainly by a grant from the Sports Council. In Wales and Scotland the equivalent body to the CCPR is absorbed into the 'Sports Council' structure for those countries.

The British Olympic Association is both the National Olympic Committee, representing British interests in the International Olympic movement, and a broader-based 'Council' with associate membership for a variety of interested sports organisations. The BOA raises money for financing the British teams participating in the Olympics and the Winter Olympics. It is also concerned in seminars for sports medicine, team preparation and management, Olympic education, and similar matters. Its members are elected by the national governing bodies for sports, the National Olympic Committee being composed of delegates from the twenty-six recognised Olympic sports.

The BOA also is served by a small number of professional officers including an Appeals Director. The latter focuses on private companies and raises considerable sums for the development of the Olympic movement in Britain. Thc BOA is concerned with both the championship and 'sport for all' sides of sport in Britain, and its membership extends from national sports organisations to individuals. The Sports Council, again, grant-aids certain aspects of the BOA's work.

The national sports governing bodies work separately more than collectively. Each is busy developing its sport at local, regional and national level. This is done through the normal procedures of international sport, namely, leagues, championships, tournaments, special events. Most governing bodies are served by professional officers whose salaries are supported, on the whole, by grants from the Sports Council, although strenuous efforts are made to generate funds independently through fees, lotteries, sponsorship and social functions. The work of the NSGBs is determined by elected and honorary officials. The larger organisations have professional national coaches to serve their cause.

Educational sports bodies have a powerful role. Traditionally the educational base has been important to British sport. At schools and in institutions of higher education, sport still figures in a way still not to be found in many other countries. A significant factor is that the student sports clubs are run by voluntary enthusiasts, supported by generous financial subsidies from the university or college authorities. Similarly in the schools. This voluntary enterprise is supported by professional back-up in the shape of Departments of Physical Education and Recreation in the higher education sector, and the physical education teaching profession in the schools.

Special interest sports organisations. The interests represented range from sports medicine, sports coaching, sports writing and recreation management, to sports for the handicapped and playing field construction.

Private sports clubs are a powerful traditional phenomenon in British sport. The majority are single-sport clubs — e.g. for cricket, tennis, soccer, rugby, squash, basketball, volleyball, swimming, etc. The multi-sport club is not yet a major factor in British sport, though the industrial sports clubs could provide a starting-point. Once school-days are past, these private clubs provide access to sport for hundreds of thousands of young people and adults.

Professional sport runs separately but parallel to the mainstream of mass sport. There are few bridges between the two. It could be said that most sectors of professional sport are parasitic, living off the main body of sport and rarely putting sufficient back into it.

Soccer is the sport most clearly professionalised. The major clubs all employ professional full-time players and support staff (physiotherapists, trainers, coaches, secretaries, etc.). They are managed much like an industry and buy and sell their commodities (players). The players are organised nationally as a 'trades union' — the

Players Football Association (PFA). The major clubs are affiliated to the Football League. Clubs outside this major sector are also organised regionally, e.g. the Southern League. In these 'lesser' leagues, players are usually part-time professionals.

Tennis is becoming highly professionalised and golf has always been so; in both cases, however, the traditional emphasis has been on the 'teaching professional' — the coach who teaches people the skills, as well as playing for money prizes. Squash, badminton, table tennis, cycling, and other sports offer a few players professional careers.

The Physical Education profession is still the womb of the whole sports movement. The teacher of physical education has the potential to fire the imagination of the child and motivate him and her towards a lifelong involvement in sport — as doer, informed supporter, sophisticated viewer, collector (of all kinds of paraphernalia with a sports theme — posters, stamps, programmes, photographs, etc.), coach, referee, organiser and passionate devotee. Traditionally, physical education specialists have worked mainly in secondary schools, but perhaps the time is ripe for them to increase their sphere of activity downwards into junior and infant education, and upwards into lifelong education. Certainly they must find a role in industry and the community in general, as work becomes a less dominant factor in the 'leisure-based' society of the future. Any society which neglects its physical education profession does so at its sporting peril.

Local Authority recreation managers are a newly developing group who administer much of the plant — the major facilities available to amateur sport.

It might be salutary to include a final factor in this summary — a miscellaneous file in which to place all those people who *think about sport*, and who do not fit into the previous categories. Of course, many of those already covered might wear alternative hats. Such people are legion; at times of critical decisions, like the selection of the team for the World Cup, the whole nation is expert on football! However, there are many who think constantly and seriously about sport. Managers of professional soccer clubs; sports film and television directors; authors; higher degree students; journalists; people who write letters to newspapers. Not enough is done to canvass opinion of this kind and, having canvassed it, to process it and endeavour to determine the collective 'opinion' about sport. There is an enormous volume of activity in sport. In addition to matches, the recreational and competitive programmes, the organisational and promotional projects, and the massive exercise of communicating news of these activities to millions of devotees all over the country and the world, there is a rich sports market. Commercial experts assess that at any one time the cash flow in the 'sports market' is of the multi-million-pound dimension.

In a truly global view of modern sport, this assessment must certainly be true. In this world context there are many different patterns of sport organisation and a rapidly developing network of relationships between the bodies who control international sport and physical education.

3

HOW SPORT IS ORGANISED THROUGHOUT THE WORLD

The organisation of world sport and physical education is also complex. There are thirteen major sectors to be considered and between these sectors the relationships are complicated. The following list is in no order of priority:

1. the International Olympic Committee;
2. the National Olympic Committees;
3. the International Sports Federations;
4. government organisations involved in sport;
5. international organisations with special interest;
6. regional and 'Commonwealth' organisations;
7. professional sports associations;
8. commercial sports companies;
9. international sports and physical education organisations;
10. sports study and research centres;
11. other organisations with a fringe interest in sport;
12. sport tourism;
13. 'umbrella' organisations.

1. *The International Olympic Committee (IOC)*

The International Olympic Committee is the guardian of the spirit of the Olympic movement. It is self-electing and its basic structure can be fairly compared to that of the Roman Catholic Church. The members act as ambassadors from the IOC to their homelands; all of them are male (although the Administrative Director, Monique Berlioux, is a woman). The IOC approves the sports for inclusion in the Olympic Games and in the Winter Olympics, selects the Olympic city six years in advance and, in general, holds the 'patent' for the Olympics. The IOC negotiates contracts with the international television companies and in the last twenty years has become the repository of substantial wealth.

In addition to the Games, the IOC manages an exciting world bank of sports expertise called 'Olympic Solidarity'; this is able to offer help mainly to Third World countries with regard to sports knowledge in coaching, officiating, administration and other technical areas. In this scheme the IOC collaborates with the different specialised sports federations (athletics, football, swimming, etc.) The IOC is also responsible for ongoing 'education' through its journal, and through the activities of its International Olympic Academy at the ancient site of Olympia in Greece. The Academy organises annual summer schools for various categories of sports, education and physical education experts. Baron Pierre de Coubertin, founder of the IOC, conceived the slogan 'Every sport for everyone'. He was concerned with 'mass' physical education as well as with the champion.

In 1973 at Varna, Bulgaria, the IOC, after a break of forty years, revived the idea of Olympic Congresses at which the meaning of Olympism should be restated to a new generation. The next IOC Congress will be held in Baden Baden in 1981, and will be earmarked as a platform for the sectional interests I am elaborating: the IOC itself, the NOCs, the International Sports Federations, governmental authorities, etc. It also falls to the IOC to recognise National Olympic Committees. The first precondition for the establishment of a National Olympic Committee is that the country in question must have at least five of its national sports bodies affiliated to the appropriate international sports federation.

2. *The National Olympic Committees (NOC)*

There is a standard 'guide' for NOCs issued by the IOC, but big differences exist in practice. Some NOCs, like the Italian (CONI), are wealthy, wide-ranging organisations employing more than 2,000 persons and acting much like a Ministry of Sport. Many are small, run entirely on a voluntary basis by a man and a dog from some obscure attic or small house. The objectives of these national committees are, however, universal. The NOCs finance and organise the national teams participating in the Olympics and Winter Olympics. They also organise events which focus on Olympism. In some countries the latter could be a week-long multisport festival — a 'national games' — and in others a mere token tribute to Olympism, such as a speech by the NOC President or the issue of a special postage stamp. In Britain, in 1979, the British Olympic Association, for the first time organised an 'Olympic Day'. Interestingly, this met with real success, and plans for future annual 'days' are well in hand. Over the years the NOCs, collectively, have felt that they should have a bigger say in the organisation of the Olympic movement. Every four years, after all, one NOC has the responsibility of *organising* the Games, and this is no mean task. Collectively the NOCs are responsible — on behalf of the IOC — for the 'Olympic Solidarity' scheme. The reasons for this are as follows: the profits from the television/broadcasting contracts for the Games go three ways internationally — a third each to the IOC, to the NOCs collectively, and to the international sports federations. The latter receive amounts proportional to the crowds they draw at the Games. The NOCs pool the majority of their share and spend it within the Solidarity framework. To the smaller countries, especially those in the Third World, the meetings of the NOCs are attractive since they illustrate a simplistic democracy — one NOC, one vote. NOCs now meet regionally (European, Arab, African, etc.) and at world level to discuss common affairs. In 1979 the NOCs of the world met as a General Assembly in Puerto Rico. The Association of NOCs was formally established at this meeting.

3. *The International Sports Federations*

In 1894 the IOC represented international sport as a whole. At that time only gymnastics, skating and rowing had separate international sports federations. Since then there has been a steady growth in the number of sports in the world and now more than 100 separate sports federations belong to the General Assembly of International Sports Federations (GAIF). These federations also profit from the 'Games' broadcasting contracts individually and collectively. As a collective body they have a headquarters and secretariat at Monte Carlo, and they meet annually to plan joint policies and to discuss issues. The international federations also organise their sport *at* the Olympic Games, in addition to their own world, regional and special competitions — at both national-team and national-club levels.

Organisationally there are again differences between the international bodies; some are structured on a one-country-one-vote basis (basketball, for example), others perpetuate an unaccountable system of graded voting with Britain perhaps getting six votes, and Zambia one vote (athletics, for example).

The GAIF, the NOCs and the IOC meet regularly as a trio at sessions of the *IOC's tripartite committee*, which is, as near as makes no difference, the heart of the world sports movement.

4. *Governmental organisations involved in sport*

The fourth element in the balance of forces in world sport is government. At the international level, 1979 is an important year for inter-governmental sports organisation. In June, the first meeting of Unesco's Inter-Governmental Committee on Sport took place in Paris. Again the basic structure of Unesco — the one-country-one-vote principle — is attractive to the developing countries. In these countries sport is developed almost entirely by government action at national and local level; there are no leisured classes and retired veterans to work on a voluntary basis.

At regional government level the Council of Europe (Western Europe) has been involved in sport for many years. It has published several documents on sports matters including the training of leaders, drug abuse in sport, and sports planning. To date there have been three conferences for Ministers of member-countries responsible for sport. There is also a permanent Committee for the Development of Sport. In Eastern Europe there are regular meetings of a similar kind, often extended to include Cuba, Vietnam, Ethiopia and other countries determined to take the 'East European road' in sports development. Both Eastern and Western Europe are represented at the European Sports Conference — a bi-annual meeting involving both governmental and non-governmental authorities responsible for sport. The Supreme Council for Sport in Africa also provides for such a meeting of state and voluntary authorities in sport and it has some consultations with the Organisation of African Unity. In Asia there are moved to establish a Council on the African lines. The Pan Arab Sports Confederation formed in 1979 brings together twenty-two Middle Eastern countries for collaborative meetings.

In all countries local governmental authorities aid sport immensely. They provide many of the infrastructures for sport and often help in leader training. They are usually responsible for maintenance of facilities — a major problem. Certainly in Britain local government aid to sport, even in financial terms, is greater than that from national sources.

The rise of governmental interest in sport has alarmed the tripartite committee, but the Director-General of Unesco and the President of the IOC are alert to the potential dangers, and are endeavouring to create permanent channels of communication — and, it is to be hoped, abundant front-line projects for collaboration. Certainly no Olympic Games or other major sporting activity at international and national level could take place unless governments of nations and governments of cities invested massively in sport. Governments thus have a legitimate point of view; they have an enormous investment in the area of sport and physical education infrastructures, and they should have a voice. They should not pick the teams. Where sport and politics collide (they do, and must, since both are part of life), only civilised conduct and astute behaviour by both sporting and governmental organisations can save the day.

5. *International multi-sport organisations with a special interest*

Outside the 'big four', there are many organisations representing specialised interests. The international student sport movement is one of the largest, and the four-yearly World Student Games are perhaps next only to the Olympic Games in size and prestige. The counterpart organisation in schools sport is not so well developed, but there are signs that it will grow at the world level — as it has at national level. World sports organisations for the handicapped are also extremely active. There are silent games for the deaf; championships for the blind in which a bell placed within a basketball and other technical devices serve as guides for the sightless. For the paraplegic and the amputee there are also international events; such sports as basketball, volleyball, throwing events in athletics, etc., are conducted in wheelchairs. Swimming is, of course, a popular event for the handicapped sportsman.

The 'Workers' sport' movement never really got off the ground internationally, although there is a small grouping in which Finland, Austria and Belgium and others are involved. Catholics and Jews also organise multi-sport meetings for their own faiths only. International military sport is another well ordered area.

6. *Regional and 'Commonwealth' sports organisations*

Regional Games started with the Central American and Caribbean Games of 1926 in Mexico City. They were designed to bring the benefits of Olympism into other continents and smaller places by increasing the numbers taking part, cutting the travel costs, and 'localising' the impact. Entries to the Olympics are dependent on the athlete reaching minimum standards, although all countries can enter one person per event by right in sports like athletics. In other sports, basketball, football, volleyball, etc., entry to the Games is by qualification. The whole Olympic operation can be extremely expensive, but Regional Games cut everything down to manageable size. There are now regional games in Africa, Asia, Central America (separately from the Central American and Caribbean), the South Pacific, the Indian Ocean, West Africa, Central Africa, North Africa, South East Asia and the Balkans. There is even an 'Arctic Games'. Some of these are 'recognised' by the IOC and are expected to observe Olympic regulations, principles and etiquette. Some cannot observe these strictly, and go their own way — a benevolent indulgence is shown by the world governments of sport.

The Supreme Council of Sport in Africa* involves both governmental and non-governmental action and has a semi-consultative relationship with the Organisation of African Unity.

Comparable to the regional games are those involving nations freely linked in cultural association. The Commonwealth Games (for 'individual' sports like athletics and swimming) are an example of these, bringing together the nations once part of the British Commonwealth (earlier, the British Empire). The growth point here is in team sports not involved in the Commonwealth Games, like basketball, which now organise their own Commonwealth championships and tournaments. Plans are in hand for volleyball and football tournaments within the Commonwealth. In this fashion the French-speaking countries are also well-organised, notably in black Africa; the French 'community' also embraces French Canada and certain islands in the Caribbean (e.g. Guadeloupe and Martinique). The Pan American Games** organisation bridges sport throughout the Americas, and there are occasional 'Socialist' sports gatherings in Eastern Europe—although the nature of these is more organisational than competitive. The Mediterranean Games are nother 'cultural' grouping in sport.

7. *Professional sports organisation*

The amateur/professional question is difficult in an international context. Some countries proclaim that they have no professionals, some international federations recognise only 'players' and ignore their fee-earning capacities, and some bodies refuse to have truck with professionals. The Soviet Union illustrates the first category, table tennis the second, and rugby union the third. In some sports the professionals do have their own organisations, however, tennis being a case in point. There has been a growth in sports management companies which control leading players.

The Football League in England is a good example of a powerful professional sports association. There is so far no sport separately represented as a real force at international level, although the Professional Golfers' Association is perhaps as near to this as any.

*Founded in 1965 by the countries competing in the first African Games, Brazzaville. Its headquarters are in Cameroon; its secretary is Jean-Claude Ganga (a Congolese) and its president is Abraham Ordia (a Nigerian).

**PASO—the Pan American Games Sports Organisation—has no permanent headquarters but moves with the election of the President and/or Secretary. It covers North, South and Central America and the Caribbean. It is non-political and includes Cuba.

Many international sports federations try to encompass the whole range of organisational forms in their sport — from schools to professional clubs. Association football is a case in point here. We have yet to find the answers, on a global basis, concerning professionalism in sport.

8. *Commercial sports companies*

There has been an astonishing growth of sports sponsorship internationally in the last twenty years. In the 1950s most sports sponsorship was discreet and gentle, mainly restricted to newspapers. As television and sport became the dual force it now is, there was a concurrent rise in the interest of commerce. Sport became fair game for the public relations and marketing men. The organisers of major international events now work hand-in-glove with commercial companies of all kinds. The Olympic movement is to the fore. Even the Spartakiade, which went international in Moscow in 1979, prided itself on the range and depth of its commercial involvement. The giant Adidas footwear company is a leader in sports sponsorship, not only directly but also through companies which it controls such as the London-based West and Nally sports promotional company. Coca-Cola is another multinational company with a big stake in sport. Television companies, of course, are deeply committed to sport in every country. As with professionalism in sport, we are aware of the problems that commercial involvement in sport creates; we are not yet sure of how they should be handled.

9. *International sports and physical education organisations*

I now wish to use the term 'professional' in the sense of those who work professionally in areas *connected* with sports and physical education. These include teachers, writers, other media people, psychologists, researchers, sociologists, doctors and coaches. These people are represented by organisations like the International Council of Sport and Physical Education, the International Federation of Sports Medicine, the International Association of the Sporting Press, the International Federation of Physical Education, and the International Track and Field Coaches' Association. There is also one association entirely for women in physical education and games.

Similar international bodies have been established to highlight outstanding examples of fairplay in sport, to bring together those in the health and recreation areas, those who train teachers of physical education, and so on. Some spawn offspring which then take on their own identity. There is no end to fecundity in this field. World sport science congresses are now a feature of the international calendar; a major congress of this kind will be held in Tbilisi, Georgia, before the 1980 Olympic Games. The sponsoring organisations for such congresses reflect and reinforce the wide variety of different organisations now active.

10. *Sports study and research centres*

Throughout the world there are now a number of these, mostly attached to, or supported by universities and colleges with a special interest in physical education. The University of Long Beach and the University of Alabama (United States Sports Academy or USSA) are two; the Institute for Comparative Physical Education at Concordia University, Montreal, is another. The Centre for International Sports Studies in London works within this growing network. These centres study international sport and physical education objectively; they also on occasions work in the international field but wear a 'national interest' hat. They usually offer two main possibilities — services and studies. Special technical services rendered by the USSA to Bahrain, for example, can realise financial profits, which can then be disposed of in the form of study fellowships.

Research in sport varies considerably from country to country. Sports medical researches have the longest history and the most obvious value in terms of injury prevention and the extension of performance levels. There are increasing numbers of professionals in sports sociology, sports psychology and sports education research. Documentation centres for sport, recreation and physical education are ubiquitous. Again they vary from the highly organised storage/translation/communication bureaux in Leipzig and Warsaw to the under-staffed, under-used 'desks', which have little more than the name, in many other countries. Easy access to information on the world level in sport is a major prerequisite for advance.

11. *Other organisations with a fringe interest in sport*

The World Health Organisation is an example, UNICEF is another. However, United Nations Agencies have decided to look to Unesco as the major co-ordinating agency for matters relating to sport at inter-governmental level. International organisations connected with health and with youth activities are obviously interested in sport. To list and categorise all these would be a gigantic task — but one which could usefully occupy higher degree students somewhere in the world. There is a growing awareness among world development organisations of the role which sport might play, especially in human resource development. At (British) national level, such bodies as the British Council, a cultural organisation; the Central Office for Information, and the Central Bureau for Educational Visits and Exchanges, have a legitimate and lively interest in sports as *part* of their general programme of work. Other countries have their counterpart organisations like these.

12. *Sports tourism*

Winter sports excursions take more than half a million Britons alone to the mountains of Europe, and there is an enormous traffic in sports tourism between countries. Increasing numbers of people choose holidays in which the major content is sport — swimming, sailing, walking, climbing, canoeing, camping. Tens of thousands of football supporters travel with their teams. The major sports championships and especially the Olympics are a spur to tourist and social development of all kinds. Hotels are urged to increase their tennis, squash and health hydro facilities to meet future tourist demands. There are abundant opportunities for sports clubs to play in international tournaments at many different levels. Town twinning schemes have a sport component: there is a growth of 'learn a language and a sport' courses for young people both in Britain and abroad. There is a growth in the keep fit movement, the slimming movement, the stay young movement. Yugoslav tourist experts anticipate that in ten years 65 per cent of their overseas tourists will be naturists.

Literally in their millions, the people of the world are turning to active tourism. Sports planning which does not consider this unstructured and massive phenomenon is not planning. Often the tourist industry can provide the sophisticated sport facilities like golf, riding and tennis — for both tourists and competitive teams — thus making big savings on the 'education' budget. This is clearly important in Third World countries.

13. *'Umbrella' organisations*

The problem with these neat organisational explanations is that they can never really represent all the forces involved. There are tensions and jealousies of an administrative nature throughout the world of sport, just as there are throughout any other social organisation. It would be foolish to expect none. Unfortunately many sports people often seem to play out highly competitive rivalries in sports administration which should be played out in the stadia and arenas — in actual sports competition.

Attempts have been made to establish bodies which bridge the differences between organisations and act as true 'umbrellas' for a whole range of interests. The International Council of Sport and Physical Education (ICSPE), established in 1960, was the last major attempt to establish a true sports forum for all voices. Unesco now gives consultative status 'A'* to ICSPE and looks to it to play a co-ordinating role in this confusing forest of assorted organisations. The IOC, the International Sports Federations and the National Olympic Committees have also considered establishing a 'World Sports Organisation'. There are a few who suggest that Unesco's Inter-governmental Sports Committee might also join it.

In countries like Sweden and Britain the lines between what is 'state' and what is 'voluntary' action, are blurred. Many organisations have the involvement and financial support of both sectors. These 'mixed economy' bodies can be found in several countries. Occasionally they meet regionally, and attempts have been made to organise international discussions. In Eastern Europe too there are 'mixed' sports administration and planning bodies. This jungle of organisations and interests baffles and preoccupies those who organise international sport. It is not easy to streamline in an area of life where so much rests on individual enthusiasm and initiative. It is not only in competing and practising where the voluntary principle holds sway, but also in coaching and administration. When we talk glibly about 'Sport for all' this should also mean 'sports organisers' and sports coaches for all. Ways and means are being found to help sportsmen achieve their best results. We need more thought as to how coaches and administrators can be helped to improve their work for sport — without becoming full-time operators. On the other hand, we also need more opportunities for those who wish to make coaching and sports administration their profession and a career. The creation of easy and efficient relationships between 'the professionals' and 'the volunteers' is a permanent and major task.

*Unesco grants the consultative status of 'A', 'B' and 'C' to international voluntary organisations. Briefly this means that 'A' organisations are those to which Unesco grants a budget and says 'get on with it, we like your programme and potential', 'B' are those that submit their programme, of which Unesco selects certain aspects for support; and 'C' are those which Unesco 'notes', for reference.

NOTE

Readers requiring a detailed run-down of sports organisations and sports centres should note the following publications:

Address book: national and international;
Directory of Sports Centres and Halls in the United Kingdom.

Both are issued by the Information Centre, the Sports Centre, 70 Brompton Road, London SW3 1EX

4

HOW DID WE ARRIVE WHERE WE ARE?

Before man emerged to higher forms of living, his physical activity was presumably based on the imperatives of hunting and being hunted. With the growth of civilisation and culture, bringing an increase in leisure, man developed systems of bodily training designed to keep him in fine physical fettle.

Even the earliest civilisations knew 'exercise'. In China, Confucius recognised that training in the arts of archery and charioteering, along with music, manners, writing, etc., in other words the arts in which a gentleman sought proficiency, had a powerful influence on the development of character. Dancing, hunting, fencing and football too were engaged in for both self-defence and worship to gods. 'The ideal of physical education in the Chou dynasty was that sports be used not only to improve the people's health but also to cultivate the virtue of citizenship and the manners of a gentleman.' The Taoists believed in the practice of gymnastics to circulate 'breaths' and eliminate internal obstacles, which can cause disease. They untie internal knots so that everything inside the organism can communicate freely. Gymnastics helped in the pursuit of the kind of bodily immortality which was the basic ideal of Taoism. Traditional boxing was practised in China from time immemorial. Those who aspired to 'transform into a Buddha' were exhorted to improve their breathing and circulation, 'hence the body should be properly exercised so that muscles and tendons will be supple and the spirit will not then suffer from the misery of weakness.'

A further advance was made by the monk Bodhidharma who, 'after sitting facing a wall for nine years rapt in meditation', invented a system of exercise known as the '18 Lo Han's Hands'; observing the 'haggard faces' of his disciples, he taught them boxing. As medicine grew in importance, exercise assumed at an early stage a 'scientific' mantle. The discoverer of anaesthetics, Hua T'o, who was also an expert in acupuncture and hydrotherapy, devised a systematic series of exercises called the 'Frolics of the five animals'. Hua T'o writes: 'The body needs exercise, only it must not be too exhausting, for exercise expels the bad air in the system, promotes the free circulation of the blood and prevents sickness. The used doorstep never rots — so with the body. That is why the ancients practised the bear's neck and the fowl's twist, swaying the body and moving the joints to prevent old age.' Hua To's five animals were the bear (strength), the tiger (power), the deer (endurance and speed), the monkey (agility) and the bird (grace and lightness). Such qualities, of course, form the basis of modern systems of training. This system, enthused the originator, 'removes disease, strengthens the legs and ensures health. If one feels out of sorts just practise any one of these frolics; it will produce sweating, give a feeling of lightness to the body and increase the appetite.'

Elsewhere in the ancient world, rules for healthy living are found in the code of Hammurabi (1,800 B.C.). In Judaism the Rabbi Maimonides drew up comprehensive rules 'to preserve bodily fitness'—some of which were incorporated as advisory into the Judaic Code of Law. In Hinduism, 'Hatha Yoga' comprised exercises which are still popular today. In the Yoga view, 'the body is the temple of the soul and must be kept healthy.' A treatise on Hindu medicine claims that 'Yoga breathing exercises are instrumental in increasing health and longevity' as well as being 'an indispensable requirement for classic achievements on the spiritual plane'. In Egypt, personal exercise came early on the scene. The chief pursuit for the young was wrestling, of which many scenes are recorded in aristocratic tombs. The history of African folk pastimes shows that wrestling was very early in fashion throughout the continent.

The civilisation of classical Greece is of course famous for its love of physical beauty and exquisite recognition of the unity of mind, body and soul. Theoretical studies on the problems of exercise are innumerable and it will suffice to mention only one. The 'Regimen for health' of Hippocrates, published in the fifth century B.C., gives high priority to exercise. 'In winter', writes Hippocrates, 'a man shall walk quickly, in summer in a more leisurely way especially if he is walking in the hot sun. Fleshy people should walk faster, thin people more slowly. Fat people who want to reduce should take their exercise on an empty stomach and sit down to food out of breath. Those who enjoy gymnastics should run and wrestle in the winter, but in the summer wrestling should be restricted and running forbidden. Long walks in the cool shade should take their place.' The Regimen has advice on the training of athletes, the place of vomiting and the importance of diet, and ends with a passionate injunction: 'A wise man ought to realise that health is his most valuable possession and should learn how to treat his illnesses by his own judgement.'

Roman writers fully realised the importance of physical health. In his *Hygieia* the famous Galen recommends exercise from an early age. He writes: 'Exercise is no small part of the art if hygiene and the avoidance of fatigue is no small part of exercise.' Ovid also has some interesting advice on how the young can attract the opposite sex: 'Men are to appear as natural as possible, glowing with health won by physical exercise on the Campus Martius, with ball games, javelin and discus-throwing, horseriding and ice-cold baths in the Tiber.' Another observer, Scipio Aemilianus, commented on visiting dancing academies: 'I swear that more than 5,000 children of both sexes were at the academies dancing with cymbals, and striking attitudes which would dishonour a slave.' The Roman citizen was extremely fond of his visit to the baths. This entailed much more than relaxation in warm water and subsequent massage. Roman baths were large health centres fully equipped with gymnasia, gardens, libraries and reading rooms. Romans went along to the baths 'to meet others, to stroll, to talk, to play ball and other games'. Some baths, like the giant ones of Caracalla, were floodlit. Unfortunately the mixed bathing sessions deteriorated into the orgies which scandalised the era of Nero — events later to be repeated in the English history of bathing when 'over-enthusiastic' bathers were disciplined by the Church.

It was Cornelius Celsus who produced the first complete compendium on health after the era of Hippocrates. In A.D. 25 he addressed 'officers and gentlemen' as follows: 'A man who is both vigorous and his own master should be under no obligatory rules and have no need either for a medical attendant or rubber and annointer. His kind of life should afford him variety — he should be now in the country, now in the town, and more often about the farm. Rest sometimes but more often take exercise, for while inaction weakens the body, work strengthens it; the former brings on premature old age and the latter prolongs youth.' Plutarch's 'Advice on Keeping Well' has a message for others. Turning aside from aristocratic hygiene, the regimen advocated for the 'idle rich' preached by the Hippocratic physicians, he says that 'health is not to be purchased by idleness and inactivity'. A man in good health should devote himself to numerous 'humane activities'.

Writers in the Middle Ages constantly associated the practice of exercise with good health. The *Regimen Sanitatis Salernitanum* had advice on all health matters. The reader is advised to 'rise early, brush the teeth, wash in cold water, and go for walks'. *The Englishman's Doctor*, published in 1608, was one translation of the *Regimen*, with appropriate comment, and purported to be 'physicall observations for the perfect preserving of the body of man in continuall health'. Sir Thomas Elyot's *The Governour*, written in 1581, is claimed to be the first discussion of the value of physical exercise to be written in England. It states: 'Continuall studie without some manner of exercise shortly exhausteth the spirites vitall and hyndereth natural decoction and digestion, whereby mannes body is the soner corrupted and brought into divers sickenessis and finallee the life is thereby made shorter.' Elyot specially urges exercise, from the age of thirteen years upwards. Wrestling, running and swimming came first in his estimation, as they 'adapt man to hardness, strength and agility'. Shortly afterwards, Richard Mulcaster made known many of the ideas on exercise expounded by the Italian H. Mercurialis in his *De arte gymnastica*. Mulcaster wrote enthusiastically on physical education himself.

Throughout the next three centuries in England there were many treatises on exercise and health including interesting works by Thomas Arnold, Jeremy Bentham, Robert Burton and others. Herbert Spencer made impassioned appeals to encourage the practice of 'the sportive activities to which the instincts impel', and drew attention to the 'physical conscience' of man. Charles Kingsley, prolific writer and professor of Modern History at Cambridge, advocated intensive courses on physical education in the large towns. Distressed by the conditions 'where tens of thousands lead sedentary and unwholesome lives', he worked hard to popularise health centres of an original kind: 'Why should not there be opened to every great town in these realms a public school of health?' He had in mind centres where instruction on all aspects of hygiene was to be given. Kingsley also called for 'corporal exercises among the students of universities'. John Armstrong, in his *Art of Preserving Health*, had written on exercise:

Of exercises swimming's best,
Strengthens the muscles of the chest,
As 'tis the best so 'tis the sum
Of exercises all in one;
And of all motions most complete,
Because 'tis violent without heat.

John Wesley was another to speak up for exercise. In his *Primitive Physick: or an easy and natural way of curing disease*, he urged the necessity for regular daily exercise. In the United States and other countries there were similar outcries.

The role of exercise in health was not questioned by those volatile 'strong men' who worked fanatically for their cause at the beginning of this century. They had no doubt that their physical efforts made them healthier and lengthened their lives. Eugen

Sandow, George Hackenschmidt and others* preached and practised their theories and converted thousands to their interpretation of a healthy way of life. Their philosophies still largely fortify the modern exponents of the 'Health and Strength' philosophy. On the continent the father-figures of mass gymnastic movements like N. Bukh (Denmark), P.H. Ling (Sweden), F.L. Jahn (Germany) and M. Tyrs (Czechoslovakia), attached deep importance to the contribution of exercise to personal health and, for political and patriotic reasons, to national health.

Another outstanding physical educationalist, also a writer, statesman and thinker, was the French Baron Pierre de Coubertin. Awarded a scholarship by his government to make a study of 'universal physical culture', Coubertin studied the role of games in English public school education; already as a youth he had spent a short time in such a school and the experience had profoundly influenced him. As a nationalist he was searching for new methods of educating the 'patriotic spirit' of young Frenchmen after his country's setbacks at the hands of Germany and its loss of Alsace-Lorraine. As an internationalist he conceived the revival in a modern form of the ancient Olympic Games. There had been several attempts to recreate these festivals, including one in England by Robert Dover whose 'Cotswold Games' lasted from 1612 till 1852 — but a real international 'Games' had not been realised. Coubertin assembled a high-powered group of sixteen enthusiasts, of whom eight were educationalists of some kind. They included Viktor Balck, the Director of the Gymnastic Central Institute, Stockholm, a Hungarian physical education teacher, the head of Russia's military schools, the Dean of a famous American university, and two Britons — Lord Ampthill and Mr Herbert, Secretary of the Amateur Athletics Association. They saw sport as a particular means of informal education, an environment for chivalrous behaviour, and a means of creating international understanding. Recognising the connection between sport and politics, Coubertin as a Frenchman could not appoint a German member to his first International Olympic Committee; one was quietly co-opted later. In his rules Coubertin recognised various sectors of discrimination which would be excluded: social, religious, racial and political.

*Sandow was a famous strong man active early this century in Britain; he founded 'Sandow's Curative Institute' in London, and called for an 'International All-for-Health League'. Hackenschmidt was world wrestling champion when he came to England (a Baltic German) in 1902, settling permanently. He wrote on sport and exercise, as well as on philosophy.

Whereas the ancient Olympic Games had a three-point programme involving sport, art and religion, the modern Games would blend sport and art. There would be competitions in sport *and* in art. In 1948 the art competitions ceased (medals had previously been awarded in a wide variety of fine arts), and 'exhibitions' replaced them.

The Games would be held four-yearly, and there was to be education in the meaning of Olympism throughout the four-year Olympiad. Olympism was, according to Coubertin, a 'wedding of mind to muscle' and a 'school for the emotions'. Olympic effort was to improve character, to display chivalry, and to search for performances that were even faster, higher and stronger. The honour was not to be only in winning; it was also to be in taking part. The underlying theme was sportsmanship and fairplay at all times. The IOC was to be the guardian of the Olympic spirit. It was a controlling body which, some say, Coubertin modelled on the Vatican and the Knights of Malta. The President of the IOC would select his sporting cardinals and appoint them as ambassadors to different regions where they would shine as beacons of Olympism.

In Britain a unique phenomenon was born: modern competitive sport. Perhaps it was due to the existence of a leisured class born of industrialisation; perhaps to the philosophy of competition which underlay capitalism; perhaps to the Protestant work ethic which ran over into play. Whatever the reasons, the British in the mid-nineteenth century began to formalise competitive sports. Often clubs were attached to factories and churches. At national level England, Ireland, Wales and Scotland played soccer in 'international' matches. In the middle of the century two English cricket teams were already touring North America. On occasions there would be handicap matches with the English eleven playing the American twenty-two.

By 1881 the first international sports organisation — for gymnastics — was established. This was followed in 1892 by international federations for skating and rowing. In 1894 Coubertin established his International Olympic Committee, and arising from his studies in comparative physical education and particularly his visits to English public schools, which impressed him by their use of sport as a means of character education. In 1889 already he was organising an international congress on physical education in Paris. In the same year the Americans had also arranged the Boston Conference on Physical Training, to assess the many competing 'systems' brought to the new continent by the immigrants — the games of the Anglo-Saxons, the gymnastics of the German

'Turners',* the gymnastics of the Slav 'Sokolists'.** Which was best for the United States? None, it was decided. Henceforth the United States was to be eclectic, choosing the best of any system, uninhibited by inheritance. Forging ahead, the Americans had established physical education at bachelor degree level by 1904. Another sixty years were to pass before Britain caught up in this particular matter.

Emigrants were taking sports to far-flung outposts. Soccer was being introduced as a palliative to Russian workers by English and Scottish factory owners, perhaps to take their minds off revolution. Football clubs like 'The River Plate' were spread throughout South America by individual enterprise of this nature. Young Englishmen brought the joys of canoeing to Germany. Young Frenchmen took rugby to the Romanians. Commercial and cultural penetration was accompanied by sports development. The colonials created multi-sport and multi-activity clubs all over the world. Imitations of Hurlingham with tennis, golf, squash, swimming, croquet and other outdoor games, together with whist, bridge, chess, drinking and tea dances — appeared in Cairo, Buenos Aires and anywhere else that the need and occasion arose (a pity their zeal did not extend to Liverpool, Birmingham and Glasgow).

At the end of the century the Oxford-and-Cambridge boat races had been established for many decades, and graduates took the sport — and business — with them to Germany and other European countries. As the Empire was extended and fortified, the British introduced their law and order, their culture — and their sports. A hundred years later, in response to a Unesco survey, the Ethiopians answered with regret that the low state of modern sports in their country was 'because we were never colonised'. Visitors to London also had the chance to study sports and physical education. At the International Exhibition of Health in 1884, a whole section and a special report was devoted to physical training.

In North America adaptations to the imported games were taking place. Baseball and softball were corruptions of rounders. Basketball began with a ball, probably a soccer ball, being tossed into peach baskets stuck on to the gymnasium wall at a YMCA centre in Massachusetts. To extract a winning shot from the basket

*F.L. Jahn (see also page 108), born in Prussia in 1778, established an outdoor gymnasium in Berlin — called the *Turnplatz* in 1811. The idea was copied in many German cities then under French domination, but in 1848 the Deutsche Turnbund was set up as part of the struggle to establish a unified German state.

**Sokol (meaning falcon) became a widespread gymnastic/patriotic movement among Czechs and other Slavs under Austrian domination. Prague Sokol was established in 1862 by Dr M. Tyrs.

the Caretaker would have to climb a ladder. The ladder was then a permanent feature of a 'goal' until someone designed a 'second bottom' with lavatory chain fixture so that the ball could be retrieved by elevating the second bottom! A simple way was finally discovered by removing the bottom of the basket: the rope structures at the base of the modern basketball ring are symbolic vestiges of that bottom which had been torn out. As the game developed in skill and excitement, it became a good spectator sport. It was played in YMCA gymnasia, most of which had balconies for the spectators. The baskets were attached to these balconies, and when the competition was hot and passions were aroused, fans would lean over and interrupt the flight of the ball. Boards were then erected to stop the fans interfering with play; only then was it discovered that a far greater variety of skill and shot was now required, since rebounds from the board had revolutionised the game situations. A game invented by a teacher of physical education for tired businessmen who could not manage gymnastics had evolved into a high-class competitive sport for giants. It was necessary to invent another one for the tired businessman. To the rescue came a descendant of Welsh immigrants, William Morgan — another YMCA gymnastics director. Morgan gave the also-rans a basketball bladder — so it is said — or perhaps an old football, and said 'Toss it about in the corner'. A rope was then erected and the group tossed it over the rope. From rope to net, from play to structured tactics, from keep fit to fitness in order to play the game itself — and another world game, 'volleyball', was born. It too was beyond the powers of the tired businessman!

The YMCA movement was a major exporter of physical education, basketball and volleyball. All over the world its 'Physical Directors' spread a particular variety of Christianity on the wings of these two games. The excellent YMCA college at Springfield was supported by a 'European annexe' in Geneva. In the USSR the seeds they planted are evident even today. The best basketballers still come from the Baltic republics — where in former times the YMCA made a strong impression. In China too there are still traces of this heritage.

Meanwhile, a group of American lady physical education teachers was visiting England. A misunderstood explanation of basketball was left behind, and 'netball' (a garbled form of basketball) was established as a game exclusively for women. And cycling for women had been made possible by the remarkable Mrs Bloomer's invention. English women seized on sport as one of the weapons with which to fight for emancipation: 'Gymnastic suffragettes' were an organised battalion ready to struggle for Mrs

Pankhurst. Struggle they did, and some are still fighting won causes: several colleges of P.E. train only women in initial teacher training colleges — Dartford, Chelsea and Bedford, for example. Deplorable examples of female chauvinism.

On the lawns of Badminton House in Gloucestershire a batting game with a feathered object — probably imported from Asia — was being developed as a diversion from tennis. Tennis itself cultivated its earlier heritage by maintaining the 15, 30, 40 method of scoring (units of 60, representing the division of the clock, being the method of counting favoured by an earlier generation), and confirmed its French roots by reinforcing the use of terms like 'deuce'. At an English public school a master — outraged at the incidence of broken windows from misdirected racket balls — said that the game could continue only if a more 'squashy' ball could be found — hence squash.

Men of Cambridgeshire and Lincolnshire, it is claimed, invented bandy at a time when the climate was more severe than now. Leisured English gentlemen like Arnold Lunn were busy in the Alps showing the locals how the utilitarian practice of skiing could be turned into a fine competitive and recreational 'sport'. The Scots developed the royal and ancient game of golf, aided by such foreigners as the Dutch organist Henry Kleek.

'Soccer' and 'rugger' factions went their different ways owing to disputes about rules, especially those on handling, in football. The Irish continued with their own varieties of kicking and striking games, refusing to be contaminated by the English interpretations. The Olympic Games had arrived in London in 1908, and someone then decided to *measure* the marathon: 26 miles 385 yards is not the distance from Marathon to Athens but that from the gates of Windsor Great Park to the White City Stadium, plus one lap the wrong way round so that the victor could pass the Queen! As late as 1974 the marathon event was still causing trouble: it did not appear in the Asian Games held in Teheran. Various reasons for its absence were given — it was the altitude, there were security problems. A more cogent reason, however, was 'Why should we, the Persians, honour an ancient Greek so-called victory?' In any case, the spokesman said, 'we made a tactical withdrawal!' One may smile, but would the French accept an invitation to an annual British athletics meeting called the 'Waterloo Challenge'?

'The Games' were underway by 1896. Not, however, without trouble and rivalry. The Greeks supported Coubertin's initiatives, expecting that the modern Games, like the old, would be celebrated every four years *in Greece*. Coubertin and his International Olympic Committee opted instead for a peripatetic Games, moving from continent to continent. For some years the Greeks then ran a rival 'Games' — but this turned out to be a futile gesture. However, the Greeks had a point: many problems in the Olympic movement would be removed if there were one Olympic city — used out of season as a United Nations University, perhaps, and supported by contributions from all member-countries.

The early history of modern sport was a series of accidents, whims and happenings. There was no one model, and no guide. Some countries saw sport as an extension of the educational programme. Some saw it as a means of perpetuating a national culture in times of oppression — a form of paramilitary organisation. The Czech *Sokol* was such a movement, and the German *Turnvereine* another. Some emphasised out-of-school 'clubs'. In many countries the 'multi-sport' club, in which the rich help the poor (e.g. the soccer section supports wrestling and handball), flourished. To get the best dinner-dance in town you had to join the sports club. In Britain the different sports developed in an insular fashion with each going its own way — the soccer club, the cricket club, the tennis club, the rugby club and so on. The principle of self-help and independence was inbuilt.

In a sense the circle has turned fully. Our new Sports Centres are certainly 'multi-sport' in conception. But they are still centres and not clubs. When the 'making it pay for itself' philosophy prevails, as regards sports centres, the user comes to be a 'throughput'. More throughputs — more money — a better report to public committee. When sport is seen as a social service, many of the dividends resulting from the public investment are hidden: e.g. how can one evaluate the saving to the public due to less vandalism which a convinced sports public for youth *might* secure? A throughput is anonymous, but a *member* gets a feeling of club solidarity by painting, cleaning and maintaining his facilities in a spirit of love. It is trying to raise the money that builds solidarity — not the amount secured.

In one area — education — Britain set a lead, if a privileged one, and became the envy of the world. The public schools, clinging to a belief in character training through the practice of sport, and rejuvenating the classical conception of harmony and balance within the mind-body-spirit trinity, influenced the state schools (especially the grammar schools) which tried to emulate them.

The British were active sports exporters but they were not afraid of importing skills when, at critical points in their history, this was needed. Before the end of the last century a two-year course, full-time, for women teachers of physical education had been established by the Swedish immigrant Madame Osterberg — brought over by a London Schools Board to introduce Swedish gymnastics. Only some forty years later did English men have their own one-year course of training — at Carnegie College, Leeds. In Scotland a course for both men and women was established at Dunfermline College but this later split into a male and female course, the women staying at Dunfermline and the men hiving off to Jordanhill College in Glasgow. There, regrettably, they have stayed and rarely do the twain meet. Just before the Second World War, Loughborough College introduced a new concept, discovered in the United States by its well-travelled Rotarian Principal, Herbert Schofield — a school of games and athletics. Schofield costed a new building with swimming pool, squash courts, gymnasium, athletics track and abundant playing fields. Too expensive, said the Ministry of Education. 'Build it', said Schofield, 'and either they pay for it or I am declared a bankrupt'. In the war, the Royal Air Force needed a centre for the rehabilitation of injured aircrew; into the breach flew Schofield again with the creation of a large additional Sports Hall with ancillary treatment rooms. After the war ended and in the euphoria of that time, the Ministry of Education and Leicester County Education Committee, together covered the main part of the account. The old man gave it the name 'Victory Hall' — was this victory in war or victory over the Ministry? Both Osterberg and Schofield were visionaries in sport and physical education; we have much for which to thank them.

After the Second World War the pattern of teacher training in physical education was simple. The women trained at the old-established Colleges of Physical Education — Bedford, Dartford, Chelsea, Nonington, Anstey, the I.M. Marsh College, and at Dunfermline in Scotland. Many studied both physical education and physical therapy. The men trained at Carnegie and Loughborough, and at Jordanhill in Scotland. Then came the delayed effect of the 1944 Education Act 'revolution in education' and the demand for a rapid and urgent flow of new teachers. For six years few teachers had been trained. Specialist courses sprang up everywhere. Birmingham University introduced a general arts B.A. degree in which physical education could be one of three subjects — this for men and women. There was a revulsion against 'militarism' and 'four straight lines', and all vestiges of the 'drill' philosophy disappeared from the teaching 'method'. Physical education had been introduced into state schools as 'drill' to keep some element of social control on children; with the social floodgates down and 'education for all' becoming a reality, the educational leaders of the early twentieth century were not all looking forward to social mobility and democracy. Moreover, many of the teachers, especially in the Public Schools, were ex-Army Physical Training Corps instructors. These brought with them gymnastics on bar, beam, rings, etc. — the 'Olympic' variety of gymnastics. At the time it was called 'German Gymnastics'. After the First World War, with anti-German sentiment still strong, some local authorities almost 'banned' 'German gymnastics'. A teacher in Erith told me some years ago: 'When the order came to hand in all "German apparatus", I hid my parallel bars under the school stage — and took them out again several years later'. While the Army had taken to 'German gymnastics', the Navy had been sold on the less competitive 'Ling's gymnastics' from Sweden. Strangely, after some exciting tours by Danish gymnasts in the 1940s and 1950s, vaulting and agility attracted the Royal Air force School of Physical Training. Until today this is still the underlying pattern of work; history encapsulated in the physical training schools of the three armed services.

The Second World War stimulated new forms of physical training, such as assault courses which were used as part of the general training of troops and as part of the special physical development courses for soldiers who were considered underweight, overweight and out of condition. These assault courses were copied as 'jungle gymnasia' for primary schools and 'circuit training' for secondary schools.

Nazi persecution brought the dancer Rudolf Laban to England in 1938: born in Bratislava in 1879, he studied art and dance, and was concerned with the national German ballet company. His 'art of movement' involved a new way of looking at the analysis of movement and its notation. He collaborated during the war in research on movement studies as they affected 'effort' in industrial work. After the war he gained the support of the Ministry of Education, directing the first state-supported course in Modern Educational Dance in Manchester, and his theories influenced the development, not only of dance, but also what came to be called 'educational gymnastics'.

There was a long-drawn-out battle over terminology. Physical training (PT), which had grown out of 'drill', became physical education (PE). Even PE was sacrificed by the fanatical 'movementiers' as they sailed through art of movement, basic movement training and human movement studies. For the sake of peace, and to enable the PE people, the dance people and the sports studies people to work happily, the term 'movement studies' is now generally accepted as the umbrella term in universities for these areas of research. This is not to denigrate the study of movement itself; there is, of course, much of deep value and interest in the study of movement and speech, movement and personality, movement and relaxation, and so on. Ironically, no more than lip-service is paid to these avenues — even by the most fanatical of the new movement specialists.

Outside the schools there is a diverse pattern of traditions. The Football Association and the Amateur Athletics Association, by their very names, assumed that they were the hub of a world movement — no need to qualify the title by the insertion of 'English' or 'British'! Their championships were *the* championships. Similarly with the Royal and Ancient control of world golf and the pre-eminent place of Wimbledon in tennis. Britain still retains the headquarters of several international sports federations, among them tennis, athletics, sailing, badminton, table tennis, cricket and part of the international rugby world. In 1976 I was able to identify more than forty individuals, citizens of this country, who hold high position in the councils of world sport and physical education (see Appendix B). It has long been so, but with sport now a world community, it may not be such a British monopoly for much longer.

In spite of rubbing shoulders with their counterparts in many foreign countries, British sports administrators remained remarkably insular. In many of these countries sport had begun from scratch, and been organised more logically within a centralised framework. And in many the National Olympic Committee was the most important umbrella for sport. It looked after the development of the Olympic family of sports *and* the others, and took an interest in schools' physical education. The NOC might even have the prestige and power of a Sports Ministry. In some it would administer vast sums of money — often from the profits made by sports lotteries and football pools. Every year an Olympic Day or Olympic Week — a national Games — would be held.

In Britain this was not to be. The British Olympic Association, established in 1905 at a meeting in the House of Commons, restricted itself to raising money for British teams taking part in the Olympic Games and the Winter Olympics. This it did effectively, largely by using an 'old boy' network. (Much can be said against such a network, but those who criticise should ensure that any system they devise for replacing it is better — and the evidence today does not show this.)

The absence of a complete umbrella body for sport and the tendency of the footballers, the rugby people, the tennis players and the others to go their own way led to the founding of a 'Central Council of Recreative Physical Training' (CCRPT) in 1935. The proposal to establish it came from two professional physical education groups, the Ling Physical Education Association and the British Association of Organisers and Lecturers in Physical Education. The name was changed in 1944 to Central Council for Physical Recreation (CCPR) and its horizons were wide, including not only sports of the competitive kind, but keep fit, country dancing, the military sports bodies, and many other diverse and quaintly British institutions. It is interesting to note that military sports organisations have never played a powerful public role in Britain; in many countries, especially where national service is compulsory, they are very important in the overall sporting structure. Britain is a notable absentee from the International Council of Military Sport (CISM). After the Second World War, the CCPR developed rapidly. A number of national recreation centres were established, e.g. Bisham Abbey and Lilleshall. CCPR regional officers did valiant work in aiding voluntary sports clubs, governingbodies at national, regional and local level, and such other bodies as sports research organisations to streamline their work.

The differences between the British method of sports organisation and that in the rest of Europe were becoming apparent; even during the Second World War there had been an Inter-Allied Conference on Physical Training. In 1948 the British Olympic Association organised a successful Olympic Games in London and the differences in approach to sport, facilities for sport, financial provision and general sports organisation were clearly evident. The first serious attempts at analysis of these differences were made by the staff at Birmingham University where, for the first time in a British University, a general B.A. degree had been structured in which physical education (sport) figured. Birmingham's publication *Britain in the World of Sport* was published and attracted the interest and concern of many. A second publication, *State Aid to Sport in Western Europe* by Dennis Molyneux, reinforced this concern. We were slipping behind our neighbours in the way we conceived and organised our modern sports movement.

First signs of progress were also to be seen in Eastern Europe. In all these countries, systematic planning was evident. Those in charge were often extremely young by our own standards; they did not inherit so many ancient pecking-orders and traditions in sport, and they were not inhibited in their approaches to such matters as the detection and nurturing of excellence, out-of-pocket payments to athletes, and the full involvement of national and local government in sports affairs. In addition (in East Germany and later in Cuba), the administrators of sport were backed up by research institutes and a system of physical education which complemented the sports programme.

There was also a games invasion from North America. Basketball was growing fast in Britain, and traditional gymnasia, crowded already with wall-bars and gymnastic apparatus of all kinds, began to accommodate the backboards and rings for this exciting new game. The volleyball development began later. Although the YMCA movement included the game in its work, and although there were little outposts around the country, especially among immigrant groups from Eastern Europe, there was no national association for the game. I first saw it played in Cyprus during my National Service in 1949. In 1954 I was appointed an assistant lecturer at Manchester University, and expected to conduct 'research': I wanted this to be practical rather than abstract work.

My interest in volleyball was re-stimulated by a group of Iraqi students at the University, who played the game regularly, and I decided to test the waters nationally. On 20 December 1954 a letter of mine was published in the *Manchester Guardian* requesting all those interested in joining a national association to contact me. Replies arrived from sailors who had played the game on aircraft-carriers, those who had seen it played in refugees camps in Europe, and from athletes who saw the game as excellent training. Three who gave the idea full support were the Director of Physical Education at Manchester University, Roland Harper; the physical director of the YMCA, Charles Pegg; and John Redfern-Collins, and in 1955 the Amateur Volleyball Association of Great Britain and Northern Ireland was created. We struggled along then on annual sums of money amounting to little more than £25; in 1979 the turnover was more than £50,000. Until the widespread building of sports halls in Britain, we were restricted to playing volleyball out of doors in adverse climate, and indoors in low-roofed buildings. By 1978, with separate associations active for England and Scotland and other regions, we in England felt able to organise the 'Spring Cup' for seventeen nations from Western Europe. The Chairman of the organising committee for this event, Peter Wardale, also officer of the Sports Council in Nottingham, was assisted by a network of more than 600 volunteers in five different venues throughout the country — a classic case of successful British pragmatism in sports organisation. The history of volleyball in Britain during the last twenty-five years encapsulates the whole range of problems faced by the British sports movement today.

5

THE WOLFENDEN COMMITTEE (1960) AND AFTER

In 1957 the umbrella body for British sport, the CCPR, appointed a small independent committee to 'examine the general position of sport in this country and to recommend what action should be taken by statutory and voluntary bodies if games, sports and outdoor activities were to play their full part in promoting the general welfare of the community. This committee was chaired by Sir John Wolfenden, and David Munrow, Director of Physical Education at Birmingham University, was one of its members. Among the problems examined were: facilities, coaching, organisation, administration, finance, amateurism, international sport, the influence of the press, television and radio, and Sunday games. Special attention was given to 'the gap', defined as 'the manifest break between, on the one hand, the participation in recreative physical activities which is normal for boys and girls at school, and, on the other hand, their participation in similar (though not necessarily identical) activities some years later when they are more adult'.

The 'Wolfenden Committee' reported in 1960 (*Sport and the Community*, CCPR, 1960). As an appendix to their report they included a summary of relevant Acts of Parliament imposing duties or conferring powers on Government Departments, or local authorities, in England and Wales in connection with the promotion of physical recreation. Only legislation affecting Scotland or Northern Ireland was not included. Among these Acts were the Physical Training and Recreation Act 1937; various Acts and other legislation affecting public authorities dating from 1890 and culminating in the Public Health Act of 1936 and the Housing Act of 1957; the Education Act of 1944, and the Acts relating to town and country planning and the countryside, of 1947 and 1949 respectively. It must have surprised many students of British sport that there had been so much government involvement in sports planning in its widest sense, even if of a passive nature. A total of fifty-seven recommendations were made relating to the problems under examination.

The major proposal was that a 'Sports Development Council' should be established. This was to be small, 'of six to ten persons', and should have the power to distribute fairly a sum of £5 million 'for the specific purposes of recreative physical activity'. This Council would be the direct link between the Treasury and the world of sport. The interest which the Wolfenden Committee had generated was manifest also in the Conservative and Labour parties. Both produced policy statements with the usual qualifications—and both published just before the Wolfenden Report itself. *Leisure for Living* was prepared by the National Executive Committee for consideration by the Annual Conference of the Labour Party at Blackpool in October 1959, and *The Challenge of Leisure* was issued by the Conservative Political Centre in August 1959.

The Conservative statement on 'A policy for sport' advocated the use of government money for the following purposes: grants to the CCPR to help it in its work and in the maintenance of the national recreation centres, 'especially for young people'; grants to the governing bodies of sports to enable coaching schemes to be improved and for the provision of more 'first-class coaches'; grants and loans to local authorities and voluntary bodies like the National Playing Fields Association for the construction of outdoor and indoor sports centres, sports grounds, running tracks and gymnasia, playing fields, floodlighting and improved changing facilities; grants towards the cost of sending representative national teams to 'prestige' events abroad (the Olympic and international football competitions were mentioned specifically). Expenditure on facilities was thought to be the most expensive item; state aid for representation abroad was seen as supplementary to 'self-help' schemes organised by the sports governing bodies, and to individual subscriptions. The Conservatives also called for the establishment of the 'Sports Council of Great Britain'. This was to be analogous to the Arts Council, established under Royal Charter as the instrument for distributing government money, and would be appointed by the Chancellor of the Exchequer in consultation with the Minister of Education and the Secretary of State for Scotland. It would 'assume the present duties of the Education Departments (in England and Scotland) with regard to sports outside the schools, etc.' It would also 'advise and co-operate with government departments, local authorities and voluntary organisations connected with the promotion of the major sports, and hold a watching brief for the less organised outdoor activities, such as hiking, sailing, cycling and fishing.' Attention was also directed to the 'confused and anomalous' position arising out of the definitions and practices with regard to amateurism and professionalism in different sports. The new Sports Council, it was thought, could have a function in moulding opinion and exerting influence towards solutions in this matter. 'Absolutely rejected' was the creation of any 'Ministry of Sport'.

Labour thinkers had applied themselves to the question 'A Nation of Sportsmen?'. A brief comparative study was included. This compared our sixty-one public cinder tracks, and seventy-five private tracks with Sweden's 800 — emphasising that there were a mere 7,000,000 inhabitants in that Scandinavian sports paradise. It drew attention to the only 10-metre diving board south of Blackpool, the general lack of gymnastic equipment, the forty-nine magnificent physical recreation centres round Buenos Aires, the splendid winter stadia in Russia, and so on. Money, it was proclaimed, was needed for both facilities and coaching. There were good ethical reasons for public expenditure on sport; the imbalance between sports provision in the public and private sectors of education could be reversed, since the great majority of young people were denied the 'classical ideal of a healthy mind and a healthy body'. It was no wonder that they behaved in anti-social ways — the failure was both theirs and society's. Much was made of this possible connection between delinquency and the lack of adequate sports provision for all. Of course it would be expensive, they said, to 'create properly-equipped centres in every industrial city, with qualified staff', but it would not be as expensive to the country 'as the consequences of social maladjustment and civic irresponsibility'.

In their conclusions the Labour people, like the Conservatives, called for a 'Sports Council of Great Britain', 'analogous to the Arts Council'. This should be 'appointed by the Minister of Education' and should include representatives of various forms of sport and physical recreation, and 'interested laymen not identified with particular forms of sport'. This Council's job would be to co-operate with the national sporting organisations in the provision of all that is necessary for the fullest advice of various kinds. It would take the necessary action to raise the general standard of games and athletics in the country and would ensure fuller British participation in international sporting events. The Council, through the Minister of Education, would be 'accountable to Parliament'.

Labour too did not believe in the idea of creating a Ministry of Sport (or of Culture). It was not necessary or desirable in Britain. Nor did they believe in political interference, nationally or locally, in the use made of the grants and facilities once they were provided. Those responsible for administering these public funds 'must be free to determine the details of their expenditure'. The Labour document had room for more specific suggestions: there would be a survey of the whole country, public opinion would be 'educated and informed' about the values of physical recreation, and there would be new attitudes towards maximum use of public and private facilities, especially at weekends. A broader base would be established for the sports-achievers, and from this base 'athletes of Olympic stature would spring up'. A serious defect in British social life would be corrected by the work of this Council: 'Youth Centres, filling the place occupied by Palaces of Culture in other countries', would be built; there would be more camp sites, more playing spaces, more swimming pools, stadia and residential hostel accommodation. In a nutshell, full use would be made of the drive and enterprise of local authorities and of the abundant spirit of service which inspires the voluntary organisations; nothing would be done to weaken or obstruct the present direct relations between central and local government. A change of outlook at the centre, expressed in a generous approach by the State, could bring 'new enjoyment and new health to millions of people'.

The direct references to 'Ministries of Sport' and State interference were directed towards potential critics. There were those who would point the finger at the worst excesses of state involvement in sport abroad — especially as the critics of Eastern Europe perceived relations between state and sport in these countries. As a partial response to these critics the Communist Party published in 1960 *Sport: a Communist Party Plan*, written by Stanley Levenson, Sports Editor of the *Daily Worker* (now the *Morning Star*). It was much more hard-hitting than the Labour and Conservative documents. The lack of facilities, the differences between sports provision in private and public educational establishments, and the need for an exciting youth service were all mentioned. Attention was drawn to the damage done to sport by speculators in land development; most sports administrators were speaking with the voice of the Establishment and lacked experience of working-class needs; the various bodies administering sports and physical education were 'in chaos' — co-ordination was 'as rare as snow in summer'. However, there were some 'rays of sunshine'. The new towns at Harlow and Welwyn Garden City were cited as positive examples, as were the sports centres at Glasgow and Birmingham Universities. Comparative comments were also included: expenditure in the Soviet Union and East Germany was quoted; Britain was at 'the bottom of the class' even among Capitalist countries — West Germany had built seventy-five swimming pools since the war to Britain's twelve, and Minnesota had 800 tracks for its population of 3 million. The Communist Party wanted the Government to implement the recommendations of the Wolfenden Report, but 'the whole of the suggested £10 million annual grant should come from the Treasury'. They disagreed with the comment on centralised planning. A 'Central Sports Council' with proper powers of control over the money was essential if progress was to replace chaos. The Council should be representative of and elected by 'the sports governing bodies, youth and educational organisations, trade unions and other democratic organisations interested in sport'. The relevant Government ministries 'should send observers'. The Council could not automatically diagnose and cure all sports ailments; it would only be effective if the sports associations, while retaining their autonomy, worked together for the benefit of sport as a whole. National control of sport should cease to be 'the prerogative of a small group of men and women'; it should become 'the responsibility of the widest sections of the people'.

With the collaboration of Regional Councils, involving the local authorities, a 'plan of national needs' could be worked out and brought to fruition. But — a great deal more than £10 million was needed. In fact, a '£100 million plan' was called for. This would start with a new look at schools sports and physical education; curricula would be wider, facilities would be freely available in school time, out of school time, and for the leaver too. Sports Centres, modelled on the Crystal Palace, would appear in every town; there would be qualified instructors. Purchase tax on sports equipment would disappear. Trade Unions were given a kick in the pants: they had 'a blind spot about sport'; they played no part in factory and office sports and social clubs, although their members 'are vitally affected'. They should 'play their rightful part in deciding the shape of things to come'. Mention was made of the world of professional sport; the large profits made from gambling and football pools; the problem of time-off for wage earners. These were important but 'less urgent than the need to provide facilities and cash for millions to take part in sport'. The aim was to help tens of millions of people to become 'healthy in mind, healthy in body'.

Nearly twenty years have elapsed since these statements were published. The Sports Council is a fact. I do not intend to make a lengthy study of the constitutional and personality problems which have bugged it from its birth, but I will try briefly to encapsulate its history by saying that the idea of a Council with a Minister as 'Chairman' has now been superseded by a Council established under Royal Charter. Although a Minister *of* Sport has certainly not materialised, we do have a 'Minister *for* Sport'; technically he is a member of the Department of the Environment and really 'Minister for Sport, etc.'. Such etceteras as drought, wintry conditions, and other Acts of God seem to be heaped upon him.

There has, of course, been substantial progress. A network of Sports Centres *has* been created in the country, thus allowing the development of such sports as basketball, volleyball and handball. Most of them are staffed by trained instructors. Our international aspirations have been facilitated by travel grants, and our sports governing bodies helped by enabling grants for professional officers, national coaches and secretarial staff. Many problems remain. At the sports administrative level there is still chaos born of administrative jealousy and rivalry. While this might be excusable internally as 'games that people play', it is embarrassing and inexcusable when it spoils our image in the international world of sports administration. There is still imbalance in our provision for the different sports, and coaching as a profession is still in its infancy.

Both the Conservative and Labour parties have been in power since 1960. In 1971 Eldon Griffiths, Under Secretary of State at the Department of the Environment, gave voice to Conservative thinking at that time. He wanted better value for money. Facilities had mushroomed, but at the same time 'magnificently equipped gymnasia, spacious playing fields, lavish swimming pools, and so on, lie unused'. Facilities belonging to schools, colleges, the armed forces and industry should, he said, be more available to the general population. He also, at this time, called for a 'new role for professional sports clubs'; unless they found a new role they might well become 'curious anachronisms playing out their fixtures in the ghostly echoes of untenanted and unwanted stadia'.

The soccer clubs could become the focal point for the community: multi-sport clubs which the whole town could identify with and support. Such sentiments were received politely in the corridors of the Football League, but action has been rare. The whole area of professional sport, spearheaded by the resource-wasting of the professional soccer clubs, has gone largely unchallenged by government. Let us consider Arsenal Stadium at Highbury. For most of the week, little of it is used except by the twenty to thirty professionals and the associated youth sides. Although right in the middle of an urban area, it is not used in an imaginative and socially useful way. The local people enter the stadium as spectators; they could continue to do this *and* have access to ongoing youth clubs, sports groups in other sports, and the sports medical facilities and expertise — enhanced to meet what would prove to be an enormous market.

In a statement to the House of Commons in 1974 the Prime Minister spoke on the Second Report of the House of Lords Select

Committee on Sport and Leisure. The question of *administrative chaos* was singled out for special treatment. It was recognised that central government responsibilities for recreation are necessarily distributed among a number of government departments and public bodies answerable to them. The time had come for the present Minister of State for Sport at the Department of the Environment to take on the responsibility for co-ordinating policies and conducting research intc active recreation. The Minister would be restyled 'Minister of State for Sport and Recreation'. His co-ordinating responsibilities would not extend to the arts, libraries and galleries; nor to the non-vocational leisure pursuits in adult and further education which remained in the orbit of the Under Secretary of State for Education and Science (the Minister for the Arts) and other Education ministers. For broad aspects of policy affecting Great Britain as a whole, the Minister for Sport and Recreation would have to co-operate with the Secretaries of State for Scotland and Wales. So much for smoothing out the problems!

In 1975, however, the Government did come out with a White Paper entitled *Sport and Recreation*. Again there was the emphasis on better administrative co-ordination in both ministerial and public sectors. In Scotland and Wales, Sports Councils had been established; there the voluntary sports governing bodies had agreed to be part of the structure as some sort of 'consultative group'. In England the old Central Council of Physical Recreation had refused to lie down and die. One of the reasons for this was a fear among sports officials, all elected, that they would be subject to the decisions of a Sports Council whose members were all appointed. Another reason consisted in the clearly evident personal clashes between spokesmen for sport in government, in the Sports Council, and in the CCPR. These were the first seeds of a problem which is currently a major sports administrative issue. The dispute was about how sport, collectively, should be organised and who should organise it.

The White Paper established a number of priorities. These included emphasis on the needs of inner urban areas; an old chestnut — the use of community facilities; a youth sports programme; the needs of the disabled; and giftedness in sport. The last-named factor has seen some practical advance in the shape of centres of excellence (dubbed by cynics as outposts of mediocrity). A recent Joint Circular from the Department of the Environment, the Department of Education and Science, and the Welsh Office treats, very briefly, the 'development of sporting talent in children of school age'.

The first statement of the new Conservative spokesman on sport,

Hector Munro, designated Under Secretary of State (Sport) in the Department of the Environment, after the general election in May 1979, was concerned with the friction between the Sports Council and the CCPR. In an article in the *Sunday Telegraph* (13 May 1979) he called for collaboration between the two bodies. 'My only worry at the moment is the disharmony between the Sports Council and the CCPR; they are so intertwined that surely we can get some harmony into this. There will be something wrong if these two cannot work together more closely.' There was also some indication from the new Minister that the Sports Council would have more say in the distribution of the public money — and the Department of the Environment less. His feelings towards the idea of the 1988 Olympic Games being in London were muted, and a final decision was left to the Greater London Council. (This great event could *force* the rival bodies in sports administration to get together. Just as the Congressional Committee set up to study similar sports problems suggested for the United States, the National Olympic Committee could be the co-ordinating peg on which collaboration could be hung in Britain. If London should get the Games in 1988, the IOC would designate the British Olympic Committee the host organising committee. This would solve, for six years, the question of 'captaincy' of the sports administration team. The Sports Council, the CCPR, the national governing bodies, the many other sports groups, and the physical education profession could use this period to overhaul their machinery and their objectives.) Should we not secure the 1988 Games the problem, of course, remains. Despite the absence of a mouth-watering carrot like the Games, we should still urgently seek a solution to a debilitating power struggle in the corridors of sport.

This, in short, is how we arrived in our present situation. The most rapid progress has been made since government, both national and local, began to take a really serious attitude to sport and physical education. In 1870 the Forster Education Act initiated an 'education for all' campaign; this would have remained a plaintive cry in the wilderness had not governments invested massively in education to make it a reality. Governments must treat sport with the same seriousness. This can be done *without* the organisations established by the state — both ministries and 'quangos' — gobbling up all existing outposts of voluntary effort and skill. All sports administrative systems depend ultimately on the tens of thousands of 'lovers of sport' who devote themselves to the movement without wishing anything more than to be useful and to be used. We should not be overwhelmed by politics and let political differences stain, and even ruin, an area where compromise and neutrality are essential. But we cannot look at the development of modern sport without thinking and acting politically; it is naive and foolish to think that we can.

6

WHERE ARE WE GOING?

There are many possibilities for the future of sport.

A wholly commercial future would mean sport becoming nothing more than a commodity to be bought and sold — degenerating at the same time into a dangerous and antisocial device. It would become a billboard for the advertisement of goods of any kind. It would be organised and directed by those for whom profit for their own business is the main motive, if not the only one.

A wholly political future would mean sport becoming the battlefield for a constant 'war without weapons'. International sport as we know it would disappear; it is difficult to envisage a world community of sport built on these frighteningly shifting sands.

A wholly technical future would entail a degeneration of the kind which is just beginning to suggest itself to us. Drugs would be commonplace; genetic engineering not excluded; the motive would be higher, further, faster — by any means and for no purpose except the blind pursuit of times, distances and medals.

We must hope that the future will be the result of balancing the new forces with the best of the old, and making determinedly creative use of what is most valuable in commercial promotion, political similarities and differences, and technology.

Certainly predictive studies are essential if we are to control the forces competing for the driving wheel of the sports movement. In most countries investment of public money into sports facilities is considerable; such investment can be of optimum value only if it is borne in mind how people's general tastes and needs might change in the future.

The three possible sports futures sketched above require more precise analysis. Sport is still discovering how to relate to commerce. Sponsorship is now deeply involved in sport, and opportunities to debate the issue are rare. Too few people are considering the ramifications. The involvement of commerce in sport — the invasion of sport by the public relations and marketing men — is extremely dangerous. Commerce can degrade and corrupt sport; the motives — and the aims — of the salesman and of the advocate of sport as education and health can be diametrically opposed. If sport is degraded in any way, it will lose its appeal to the youth of each generation, who in the past have turned to it for selfless struggle and inspiration.

Secondly, the involvement is not efficient. Companies aim to gain maximum sales for their products; to do this they select sports which are likely to attract television coverage. To associate their product with a minor sport is not worthwhile from their point of view. Even if their aim is not to increase direct selling, they exploit sport as a means of achieving social approval. For example, tobacco companies use sport to secure social approval for the habit of smoking, while health educators and, increasingly, governments are trying to make the habit of smoking appear abnormal, not normal. For those who organise and direct sport to dodge this issue is completely hypocritical. Thirdly, the involvement delays the necessary government action which will determine whether the sports movement will be balanced, whether sports for all will be an actuality or merely a slogan, whether those with talent will be nurtured. Here arises the somewhat vague question of how companies manage to divert large sums into sports budgets. Presumably such payments are allowed against tax as justifiable marketing and publicity. Hence they are not usually made out of profit. They are not a 'free gift' (the only truly free gift is the anonymous one). They are a commercial *investment* in sport.

All this does not mean that there is no place for the involvement of commerce and industry in sport; but it is meant to underline that sport should not depend on such sources of revenue for its very life. There is much to be said for the association of sport with major industries; I am sure that Derby County Football Club and Rolls-Royce Derby could establish a liaison which would do good to the club by broadening its scope and to industry as being likely incidentally to improve industrial relations (provided, of course that Derby stayed on a winning run!). The involvement of West Ham with Ford Motors at Dagenham is another obvious case where there could be twinning; wherever there is a major industry in a town, there could be a deliberate and massive tie-up. There is a growing involvement in sponsorship by local authorities, and sports equipment companies of course have a right and proper interest. Travel companies are another category of commerce where there is an obvious mutual interest; without the possibility of easy and cheap transport there would be no national and international competitive sport worth speaking of.

The first ethical hurdle to overcome in thinking about this problem is whether we want sport to remain primarily a 'school for valour and chivalry' or whether we are content for it to become just one more area for commercial exploitation. Few of us would agree that *any* area of life should be wide open to the salesman. Where do we stop? Should the helmets of policemen on duty be available as advertising space? On the sides of the warships of the Royal Navy? And what about churches and education? I think most of us would feel uneasy if the church we attended were openly sponsored by trading stamps, and would not want children's education to depend on the financial support of soft drink manufacturers. For those of us who still believe in sport as a social service, a school for the emotions, a wedding of mind and muscle, a human right — the unfettered involvement of commerce would be an insult.

There are also the feelings of the individual sportsman to consider. Is the sportsman to be seen as an unthinking circus animal or as an intelligent, educated, balanced human being? If we assume the latter, it should be recognised that the regulations of some international sports federations concerning sponsorship are impertinent. The name of the sponsor is generally written in large letters beside the vest number in athletics — a clear target for the television camera. This was never the case twenty years ago when athletics sponsorship was restrained and dignified. Athletes today seem compelled to accept sponsorship; yet they are not in a position to make a reasoned decision about a product. As an athlete I might want to stand up and be counted regarding vegetarianism, the needless processing of cheese, the value of herbal as opposed to chemical health products, and so on.

This lack of choice detracts from the major advantage of sport in society — its role as a means of informal and complete education and as an agency for health. But perhaps the consensus of opinion is that this should not be its role any longer. Perhaps the world is happy that the top Wimbledon stars should become millionaires while the public tennis courts stay bare of coaches. Perhaps we are unworried about the behaviour of some of these 'prima donnas' and their influence on young people in sport. Perhaps there is no provable connection between making sport a commodity, the 'professional foul', and violence on the field and on the terraces. But there *are* links between the factors in this chain. If as much time, effort and money were spent on publicising ethical behaviour in sport (playing and watching) as is spent on selling beer, we would all feel happier about the future of sport.

But commercial sport is with us. Can we control it? Can we establish categories of sports sponsorship? Are there some products that are so much the antithesis of all that sport stands for that they should never be associated with it? Are there some which are clearly rightly and properly to be linked with the practice of sport? Are there some which are entirely neutral and could be attracted so as to give sport a helping hand? What leadership is being given to sport in this matter? Where are the think-tanks and advisory bodies that are considering this question? I do not see them, nor do I read their reports. But I do see commerce steadily encroaching on sport at the highest levels. If it can be claimed that a certain product rots children's teeth, I want that claim examined and answered publicly. Until that is done I am uneasy about supporting a sports-product link. I cannot fight on all fronts at the same time so I must choose my target. Tobacco *must* go — and others might get the same treatment later!

Of course life is full of compromises. Many people do not share my view of this problem. In many mixed economies sport has already sold its immediate future to commerce. There are some positive results. The sports movement has discovered that it provides tremendous television entertainment. Sport is beginning to market itself properly. The Olympic Games in Moscow is 'sold' for more than £100 million, which the Olympic movement puts to good use — much of it into the exciting world bank of sports expertise called 'Olympic Solidarity'.

Let me say finally that I have no objection to commerce or to profit — on certain conditions. And I have no objection to patronage in sport. However, I do object to the abject surrender of sport to market forces. I want sport to maintain a moral leadership in the world. I want interested commercial agencies to observe the ethics of the sporting message and the principles of sport as health and education.

Now for the political future of sport. Coubertin was wise to establish four categories of discrimination in sport: social, religious, racial and political; these four are expressly outlawed in the Olympic rules. Social discrimination is fast disappearing, and in our society it is fair to say that the majority sports have seen the last of it. However, it lingers in tennis, where membership of the All England Club seems not to rest on ability alone and where membership of the national teams seems to be dominated by a few tennis dynasties (e.g. Mottrams, Brashers, Lloyds). It lingers in riding where ownership of a stable of ponies might be a social as well as an economic problem for people in Bermondsey. It lingers in skiing where residence in the Alps for several months a year could also be difficult for some. The nature of some sports means that this problem will always be with us.

Religious discrimination lingers in some countries. It affects the participation of women in sport — and it is interesting to note that Coubertin did not have a category for sex discrimination in sport.

But, again, the impetus has been powerfully towards eradicating religious discrimination.

Racial discrimination is acutely with us. It poisons international sports relationships, and threatens to spoil yet another Olympic Games. In South Africa the colour of a man's skin prevents him from playing in sports with his fellows and from representing his country. An abomination, of course, but how much evasion and hypocrisy the South African question has evoked! I ask those who try to excuse white South African behaviour to do a few small things when they think about this matter: imagine you are black yourself; try to bring one black person into your discussions; refer always, honestly, not to 'South Africa' but to 'White South Africa'. In sport there should be no compromise with apartheid. True breakthroughs can be made. Abraham Ordia, President of the Supreme Council of Sport in Africa, once said to me: 'my critics say I want to bring down the whole structure of South African society, using sport as my weapon. They forget my attitude to Mozambique and Angola when they were colonies. In these countries the Portuguese did not discriminate *in sport* and we played against them without problems.' The essential ethic of international sports relationships is selection on merit, and apartheid flies in the face of this. To excuse sports apartheid by pointing to abuses elsewhere, however great, is hypocritical.

When I read that a Welsh rugby team has just left to play in South Africa, leaving behind a black player who elected not to go, I can hardly believe any more in *esprit de corps* through sport. Why do they want to go anyway? Is the tourism more important than solidarity and comradeship? Must the black player accept honorary white status? Must he play to segregated audiences? Must he be unable to dance with a white girl at after-match socials? The exclusion of white South African teams from international sport has done more to change the situation than any amount of so-called 'bridge building'. Once the white minority suffer the *total* exclusion from the international sport movement which they have willed on their black majority permanently, they may begin to make the basic changes which are needed for them to be received again with acclamation into sports civilisation. Even today Britain is still respected as the home of justice and fairplay; tragically, we are seen to be unwilling to stand up and be counted on the issue of racialism in sport. Again, however, the currents of change are in favour of the Olympic hope — racial discrimination will go.

We are left with political discrimination, the most difficult to deal with. It spreads across the others, and is the one most difficult to define, identify and control. It was once summed up by Philip

Noel-Baker, great sportsman and Nobel Peace Prize winner, when he said that both sport and politics were part of life. Because of this there would be moments when they meet; at these meeting points there would be problems, which could be solved only by civilised behaviour and observance of the principles of human rights. In his structure of the first International Olympic Committee, Coubertin foresaw political problems; he invented 'athletics geography' in order to justify the inclusion of a Czech and a Hungarian — but no Austrian despite Austria's political supremacy within the Austro-Hungarian empire. In the early Games there were quarrels about the order of marching! For example, should Finns march behind the Russian flag? British-United States problems were highlighted by the disqualification of an American runner in the 400 metres. (The American runner in the 400 metres defeated the Briton; during the race the British judge had been exhorting his compatriot through the loud-hailer; when it was clear that the American was about to overhaul the Briton the judge then cut the tape and disqualified the American for 'barging'. It was ruled that the race should be run again the next day but the Americans departed in a huff — justifiably, by all accounts. *The Times* reported that the British had taught the Americans a good lesson in fairplay!)

In 1920 the Belgians refused outright to invite the nations which had fought against them in the Great War, just ended. Coubertin felt it was technically wrong, but he 'understood' their feelings and saw no reason to insist on the participation of those nations. He was a great pragmatist and politician: he knew that the major task of the International Olympic Committee is to ensure the participation of the vast majority of nations — even if a few are unfortunately excluded. The worst result of international sporting-political quarrels would be if the world sports camp were to become split into two blocs. In 1948, of course, Germany and Japan did not appear in London, the official reasons being that they did not have Olympic Committees at that time! The first international athletics match between Britain and France ended with the British bus being stoned by a French crowd because the franc had been devalued on the British currency market. In 1956 much space was given in our newspapers to Hungarian-Soviet battles fought out in the water-polo arena; less was given to the refusal of the Greek team to give a proper salute to Prince Philip so as to record their displeasure over the Cyprus problem. Throughout the history of the modern Olympic Games there have been problems. At no time has it been subjected to the heavy hand of absolutism; the hope of full international brotherhood has always been a *hope*; regulations have never been enforced with a finality suitable only for prisons or law courts. As Lord Killanin has said, 'Everything one does is seen by half the world as too fast — and by the other half as too slow'.

Lord Killanin's own home, Ireland, makes for a fascinating study. In rugby and many other sports, Irish teams are selected from the Republic and Ulster together. In athletics and soccer they are separated. A great deal of latitude is accorded to the Irish in these matters. An Ulsterman, if he wishes, can win a medal for Ireland — not Great Britain — in the Olympic Games; an exemplary modern example of 'athletics geography'.

We have before us in world sport today the problems of China and Israel. In Olympic terms, China was humiliated at one of the weakest points in its history, after a long and bitter revolution, when the headquarters of its National Olympic Committee was moved from the mainland to Taiwan. A team from Taiwan, with all the trappings of independence, constantly appeared in international competitions. I wonder how we in Britain might have reacted in 1945 had a group of British fanatics, sympathetic to Hitler, occupied the Isle of Wight, terrorised the indigenous occupants, and set up national teams purporting to belong to the 'Free Republic of Britain'. I doubt if we would have seen it as part of the democratic process; rather it would have seemed an intolerable provocation. The 'China question' seems now to be near a solution; certainly the feeling is no longer that a majority must suffer, and in the Asian Games Federation at least anyway it has been determined that China's seat must be held by the mainland.

In the case of Israel, sport is faced with an almost insoluble problem. The great majority of Arab countries recognise Palestine. They feel as strongly about this — and the hot war which the question has generated in their part of the world — as we once did about the Germans and the Japanese. To them the presence of an Israeli team is a provocation. But Israel is a state recognised by the United Nations and by the International Olympic Committee. In some sports the Israelis take part in international competition as part of 'Western Europe'; in some events, like the Mediterranean Games, they are not invited — the guest list being decided by the organisers. With the coming of a national home for the Palestinians — perhaps as soon as the 1980s — we will see Palestinian sports teams in international competition; already Palestinian applications for recognition by international sport federations are being received.

It is important to study these questions from a truly international viewpoint. In the African Games in 1978, at Algiers, there was much play in the soccer tournament on the unfortunate squabble between Egypt and Libya. This led to the early return of the

Egyptian delegation — on the initiative of the Egyptian Minister of Defence, who was startled by the pictures and commentary he saw at home on television! Little publicity was given to the positive elements of these regional Games in terms of international relations. Morocco had appeared in Algeria despite the absence of diplomatic relations between the countries. Egypt had already played Algeria at soccer despite the underlying political tensions between Egypt and a 'hardline state'. Somalia had played Ethiopia at table tennis; a match which ended with the Somali ambassador accepting defeat gracefully in the sports hall and inviting the Ethiopians to a return in Mogadishu — another example of ping-pong diplomacy. At the Asian Games in Bangkok in 1978 the North and South Koreans actually played against each other in the soccer final; they stood for a group photograph together, and even shook hands. In the Central American and Caribbean Games there is an almost permanent sports-political anomaly. The French territory of the Antilles (Martinique and Guadeloupe) is not allowed to compete since participating nations must have 'independent Olympic Committees'; they are 'parts' of the French Olympic Committee and thus debarred. Those British colonies that still survive (e.g. Hong Kong and Belize), having independent Olympic Committees, are allowed into their regional games.

There are no easy solutions to these problems and those who have to try to solve them deserve our sympathy and support. Furthermore governments do have valid opinions and these must also be respected. If a government sees its country's image about to be devalued in world opinion by sports groups who feel they have no responsibility to anyone but themselves, it has the right to act (as the French and Irish Governments did in September 1979 over the proposed South African visiting team based on a three-colour structure). When sport behaves according to its highest moral principles, *most* governments still respect its neutrality and make astonishing compromises with their own political principles. When sport acts in a squalid manner — as in rationalising apartheid — it should not be surprising that governments intervene. Those who work in sports-politics can only observe the generally-held principle that they apply the art of the possible — and sometimes even the impossible.

I venture some thoughts for the future on this question. Can sport not return to some earlier and basic hopes? For example, could international sport be a manifestation of national *cultures* and not national governments? Could the neutrality of the Olympic city be truly observed — for a period of a month could it not be 'free' territory? Can we now allow host cities more flexibility, especially in regional games, to exclude from the invitation list countries which, at that particular time, offend a majority of the other guests? This is the case at present in the organisation of the Mediterranean Games; a two-thirds majority, I am told, is required by countries wishing to participate. If only countries would realise when they are in this position and not use sport almost maliciously to promote their political viewpoint, at great cost to others, insisting on their 'right' to attend. Is the 'mongrelisation' of international sport, as in the World Athletics Cup, an answer to sports-political problems? New Zealanders, when absorbed into 'Oceania', did not offend Black Africa.

It is depressing when the Olympic village becomes an armed camp: is the Olympic movement, then, any longer worth all the effort and the hope lavished on it? There must be a better way. Nevertheless, in spite of all this the future of the movement is still promising. Every Games has been said to be the last! We know that Los Angeles will organise in 1984, perhaps London in 1988; Cali wants to be the first South American city to host the Games, and might bid for 1992. The Greeks have already started building a new Olympic complex in Athens to celebrate the centenary of the modern Games in 1996 — and who could deny them that honour? Will Peking be willing to wait until 2000 or will it bid earlier?

And so to the technical future for sport. What can science offer us? William Johnson, an American writer (writing in *Sports Illustrated* 23 November 1974), sees the future of American sport, competitive and non-competitive, as fitting into two broad scenarios — *technosport*, that which is the product of machines and technicians, and *ecosport*, that which springs from the natural relationship between man and his environment. Although these are in a sense opposites, they could easily co-exist in the world of tomorrow in which 'pluralism' (that which allows nearly everything to exist with nearly everything else) would be the dominant characteristic. Technosport would bring with it more 'technological fixes': football players will be so padded that they will look like robots; 'jock* breeding' might become common; the world of 'Roller ball', in which aggressive sports take the place of war, could be on the horizon.

Technosport stadiums would be grand monuments — domed, artificially turfed, airconditioned, illuminated; they would be equipped with push-button vending machines at each seat; individual TV replays which can be punched up at will; people

*Americanism — a person interested only in sport. A male jock would marry a female jock ...

will be led to their seats by the rustle of leaves, the babbling of brooks and other sounds of nature. The structure of the stadium will be changed as various parts are moved on air cushions. Computers will be common; they will be used to find partners in a new locality for golf, squash or tennis. They will be used for gambling; trainers and coaches will call on them for probability forecasts. Spectators will be brought closer to the game by electronic devices so wired as to bring players' conversations, yells and groans, the sound of body collisions, etc., directly to the individual fan. On 'Brave New World' lines there will be electronic sensory perceptors enabling the fan to experience the pain, the emotion, the exhilaration of sports without moving a muscle. Some way-out thinkers envisage total spectator-participation in team selection and tactics. Each fan would have his own computer wired to a central club unit; decisions on selection and tactics would be decided by majority vote!

Ecosport would represent the other extreme. Technology and artificiality would be abhorred and disdained. Its games would be new, without boundaries perhaps, flowing and free. Victory would be muted, perhaps even abolished. Everyone would participate; sport would be integral to the ecological movement and conservation. Man would be central to ecosport; in technosport man would be part of the machine.

The position of aggressive sports like boxing will become a good guide to the 'eco'-'techno' debate in the future. Some defend boxing as a safety valve, an argument countered by those who say that hitting the punchbag gives the same relief as hitting another human being. The issue is debated by numerous medical 'experts', few of them neurologists. I have yet to read a neurologist claiming that blows to the human brain are of little consequence, or that brain damage is anything except irreversible. I am of the simple opinion that intentional damage to the brain, the eyes, the mouth, the face and the nervous centres of the body cannot be termed 'sport'. We have invented many ways of testing courage; against the elements — mountains and water — by lifting weights, by throwing implements, and so on. We even have combat sports like wrestling of which the rules prevent brutality. We have fencing, in which the danger has been eliminated by electronic devices. Is there anything to stop boxing — for which, I agree, the training is superb — from becoming ritualised into symbolic conflict — just like fencing or like Chinese boxing, Tai Chi? If man evolves in the future it will not be in his body but his mind. So why set out deliberately to damage the repository of his mind?

The 'human growth and development' movement, springing

mainly from the Esalen Sports Institute in California, indicates the moves towards ecosport. Sport is seen as a means to achieve self-discovery. Tennis becomes Western man's Zen. Buddhist and other oriental philosophies are re-aligned, re-discovered and applied in a sports context. With high-powered competitive sport stressing 'switching on', ecosport will emphasise 'switching off'. Through sport, man of the future will strive for self-realisation; he will use sport to transcend consciousness.

An East German writer, B. Musiolek, sees an increasing desire for participatory sports along with the raising of educational and cultural levels everywhere (in 'On the future of physical culture and sport', *Olympic Bulletin of the DDR*, IV, 1970, in English). The socialist countries will encourage the desire for regular physical exercise; there will be increasing inter-relations between work, leisure-time activities, education, health, holidays and living conditions. The future will be shaped not by robots but by 'active, working, creative individuals'. Anatoli Korobkow (in 'Sport in the year 2000', *Journal of the International Sports Medical Federation*) speaks of sport becoming 'pharmacology for the healthy individual'. It will become part of a health programme designed to immunise the organism against many of the stresses of city living and new 'diseases of civilisation' (e.g. heart attacks). Special exercise programmes will be worked out to suit different occupations; workers on the skyscraper blocks, now common in all cities, will concentrate on acrobatics, climbing and slalom racing. As life below water and in space passes from the extraordinary to the commonplace, man will be permanently prepared for such changes by appropriate training.

Professional forecasting on an international scale has little to say directly about sport but much about society in general. There are some interesting examples of successful predictions. Aldous Huxley foresaw the whole drug scene, H.G. Wells the space age, and Orwell the political power-blocs. Even cursory futurology presents some fascinating possibilities for sport and physical education.

Herman Kahn, through his Hudson Institute, is perhaps the most renowned of modern futurologists. He foresees, after two decades of malaise in the 1980s and 1990s, a 'new era of unbounded prosperity' dawning with the twenty-first century. After the year 2000, barring serious bad luck or mismanagement, people all over the globe will enjoy 'nearly universal abundance'. This is a more optimistic forecast than some that Kahn has made in the past, and contradicts the latest predictions of another famous futurology think-tank, 'The Club of Rome'. This foresees a growing world population competing for, and depleting, the world's supplies of food, energy and space for waste disposal. Kahn dismisses this argument as 'currently fashionable conventional wisdom', but agrees that we are in for some shocks before most of the problems will be brought under control. He thinks that the very urgency of the problem will stimulate man's capacity to solve it. This, he says, is borne out by a study of the history of science and technology in the nineteenth and twentieth centuries. We should develop 'positive images of the future' to counteract a widespread 'failure of nerve' among the world's influential people. Man at play, man as sportsman, man as muscular animal, can contribute to these positive images of the future.

In 1971 the Hudson Institute was asked to make forecasts up to A.D. 2025. It came up with five main trends:

1. *Biomedical*: there would be a growth in spare part surgery, genetic engineering and in the field of anti-ageing.
2. *Behaviour control*: there would be more chemical intervention and the use of brain electrodes in controlling the behaviour mechanisms of man.
3. *Computers*: more people would have personal data networks; automation and electronic 'thinking' would be commonplace.
4. *Environment control*: exploration of the continental shelf for more than oil and gas would be common; weather modification would be advanced.
5. *Exploration of space* would develop.

The ramifications of the first of these trends for sport have been spelt out already, but it might be useful to reinforce the relation of exercise to anti-ageing techniques. There is one school of thought which points out the dangers of sports skills — for example, the increase in arthritic conditions arising from old sports injuries. The overwhelming feeling is still, however, that appropriate sports and exercise keep men and women younger longer. The second trend is immense in its potential in all areas of life. The third has been discussed as an aspect of 'technosport'. Environmental control in a limited way is already in action: artificial environments for ice skating are now found in the tropics; plastic surfaces are used for ski training and ice hockey; night becomes day in sports halls. Man conquers space by creating biological efficiency before orbit and maintaining it inside the capsule.

Forecasting in education has obvious relevance for physical educationists. A 'European 2000 Committee' came up with four possible futures for society. It saw the development of the neo-industrial society, the social welfare society, the compulsory-collective society and the voluntary-collective society. The first was typified by the thinking of Edward Heath, the second by that of

Harold Wilson, the third by contemporary Chinese policies, and the last by Ivan Illich. Illich of course has been of profound influence in challenging the convergent thinkers. His 'Deschooling Society' set educationists back on their heels. His theories are meant to show that the gap between those who go to school and those who want to but do not go will *widen* in the Third World. New ways of reaching children must be found; educationists must become innovators. The traditional school is not the only answer; teachers, like other professionals, must stop sheltering behind the protection of 'diplomas'. Ways must be found of helping people become self-reliant in medicine, in transport, in agriculture, and in education. This thinking ought also to alarm and inform hardened sports bureaucrats.

The 'Heath model' may be what we should expect in the next five years in Britain: sport being asked to 'stand on its own feet' and pay for itself, forced to act like an industry in an era of cutbacks in public expenditure — abandoned to market forces, perhaps? The 'Wilson model' might have been for more public involvement in sport, municipalisation of the professional soccer clubs which would be transformed into multi-sport clubs, sport treated like a necessary social service comparable to the health service. The Chinese model is now tarnished by sudden and remarkable changes in direction, but 'Friendship first, competition second' shone like a beacon to the rest of the world and was a salutary reminder of 'what sport is really all about'.

The German novelist Günter Grass also makes a significant contribution to this debate ('Fleeing towards the future', *Encounter*, February 1979). He is worried by the dominance of 'those who know' — the intellectuals. He reminds us of the clearing of the Janatha colony in Bombay — a gigantic slum of 70,000 people bulldozed to make way for a nuclear research centre (responsible for India's first atomic bomb). The Janatha colony was moved to land which is liable to become swampy; in the first months several hundred children died and suicides increased. Meanwhile the nuclear plant organisers built tennis courts and golf courses on which the scientists could unwind. They feel secure, enjoy their research, and are among the new élite. They are 'those with heads too large in which is devised that which points beyond man and his slum horizon. It all depends on them. They are precious. The future belongs to them.'

When I read this I think of Isaac Eli, a former student at Loughborough University, the only truly qualified physical education teacher for twenty years in the Southern Sudan. He served an area bigger than England, Spain and Germany together. His flock speak many languages, are mostly pastoral tribes and number some 4 million. They have been overwhelmed by war and by refugees from other wars. What future is there for them — this year, next year — in the context of these theoretical deliberations?

There are many other straws in the predictive wind. Pierre de Coubertin hoped that the Olympic movement would have an office for this very purpose, and indeed he established the Bureau International de Pedagogie Sportive in Lausanne fifty years ago. Its main purpose was to be a 'weather vane' pointing out the directions in which sport might move. The trends for change in Olympism are themselves an interesting pointer to the future. Happily the most enterprising features of modern Olympism are concerned with the wider educational and social messages of the movement — the revival of the Fine Arts sectors, for example — and the development of 'Olympic Solidarity', which is a North-South dialogue endeavouring to eradicate the existence of 'haves' and 'have nots', in the family of world sport at least. Olympic host cities ponder on the problems of organisation; how to make the Games contribute to the long-term development of urban recreation and not merely be a showpiece event which needlessly drains the public purse for generations to come. The rise of the regional games in Africa, Asia, Latin America, the South Pacific and elsewhere suggests that one possible future for the Olympic movement could be more regionalisation with 'grand finals' taking place every four years.

The Olympic Congress at Baden-Baden in 1981 follows the Congress of 1973 in Sofia. Such Congresses were invented by Coubertin as a means of teaching to each generation the true meanings of Olympism. The original meetings were concerned with such topics as 'sports psychology' and 'sport and the cinema'. Before 1973 there had not been a Congress for forty years — a sad testimony to the thinking of the incumbent members of the International Olympic Committee. One of the major themes for the Baden-Baden Congress will be international collaboration in international sports organisation. Currently the IOC, representatives of the National Olympic Committees, and delegates representing the International Sport Federations, meet regularly to plan policy. This is the 'Tripartite Commission' of the IOC. People in sport are asking whether this will now become the 'Quadripartite Commission' by the inclusion of representatives from Unesco's Inter-Governmental Committee on Sports.

Another possible administrative future for world sport could be based on regions. The Supreme Council of Sport in Africa is a powerful regional organisation; it represents both voluntary and state sports organisations, discussing and co-ordinating policy and action. There are moves to develop the Asian Games Federation into a similar all-powerful body for that region. The Pan-American Sports Organisation has identical thoughts. Could the pinnacle of world sports administration be formed by leaders of these regional bodies? If so, Europe lags behind. There are no European Games. Some European countries feel they already have too many international engagements, and would like less — probably not a feeling shared by the practising athletes. The Council of Europe has a sports committee, and the East European Sports organisations have occasional meetings. At true European — all-Europe — level there is the European Sports Conference; at the moment this is a low-profiled assembly of people and opinion but could be 'upped' in importance.

It was Coubertin also who first conceived that élite sport and mass sport are ends of the same spectrum. Being complementary to each other, both are necessary. Mass sport today is reflected in tourism. Much old-style tourism was 'holiday plus gambling'; modern tourism is 'holiday plus sport'. Millions of people devote their vacations to the sunning, the watering, the hardening and the pampering of their bodies. Tourism grows incredibly. There are migrations from Lancashire to Majorca, from Poland to Bulgaria; weekends in Moscow and Budapest as well as in Paris and Madrid can be enjoyed by Britons. No part of the globe is out of reach.

A positive trend is that towards naturism. Southern French beaches are often topless; Americans talk excitedly about nude beaches in Mykonos; Germans have already quietly organised naturist beaches in the Canaries. The naturist holiday has been best developed by the Yugoslavs for whom statistics show that by the end of the 1980s 65 per cent of their tourism will be naturist. Every major Adriatic resort has a naturist beach or island. John Flugel foresaw this trend many years ago (*The Psychology of Clothes*, London: Hogarth Press, 1950). After explaining how clothing had developed for three reasons — first for decoration — the wearing of chains and beads for decorative purposes; secondly for protection against the elements; and thirdly for reasons of modesty — he predicted that with changes in moral codes and religious belief, and with better control over the environment, the last two would disappear in reverse order. The topless beach is with us; the naked beach is round the corner — for everyone. Will we return to the 'naked art' which was gymnastics for the Greeks of antiquity?

What is now a possibility for all has been the privilege of a few for many years. It is not enough to intellectualise the naturist (or nudist) movement. One has to experience the freedom and joy of a naturist centre to understand it. Sport for all, family sport, has been part of the naturist movement for a long time. That this should be common knowledge only now illustrates how biased the media has been towards this social phenomenon. In Britain, a small group of people held on to the notion against all odds. They were odd-bods, and psychiatrists elaborated bizarre explanations for their behaviour. The common man, brought up to experience nakedness in the presence of the opposite sex only as readiness for the sexual act itself, wondered how nudity in other contexts might affect him — for all to see. It is astonishing how nakedness can liberate; how it disarms the aggressive. The democracy of nudity is best demonstrated in Finland where the first item on the agenda of sports conferences is 'Sauna'. Subsequent sessions are conducted without false pride!

The naturists have for many years provided for themselves, at low cost, sports facilities to be used the whole year round. They work physically on these facilities. Members representing a great diversity of skills and trades give their services free. Often there is a relaxing role reversal: the solicitor digs the trenches; the teacher paints the fences; the postman acts as secretary. Mum plays mini-tennis while Dad prepares lunch on the camp site. Volleyball, five-a-side and *pétanque* (French bowls) are provided for. Many centres have excellent swimming pools and some have saunas for winter use. Fifteen miles from Charing Cross, in Kent, stands one of the best of these naturist centres. Those who talk about 'sport for all' should take a look at naturism. I feel sorry for the hordes rushing to the Kent coast at weekends while the naturists really *live* in a forest at Orpington. The orthodox resistance to the naturist movement would be laughable were it not tragic. With or without clothes, the concept of small sport and recreation units — on a do-it-yourself basis — are, I suggest, the most appropriate to societies trying to handle the problems of stressful, intensive, urbanised living.

Naturists concentrate on living for the whole family. Infants can be reared as they should be — freely in nature and with abundant playing facilities. Those who live in high-rise flats can rent camping sites. Young people can see the opposite sex totally naked and not suffer inhibitions of a visual kind. Naturists have anticipated tomorrow — and their tomorrow has a powerful chunk of sport in the overall package.

Sports fashions are held by many to predict general fashions of the future. The miniskirt at Wimbledon worn by Suzanne Lenglen over forty years ago heralded the miniskirt *en masse*. The hacking jacket became the sports jacket for ordinary wear; will the track suit too become normal street dress — if it has not already done so?

As we become a nation of walkers, joggers and cyclists, will not such changes in dress become essential? Some forms of dress enable people to experience the 'feel' of occupations which will never, for practical reasons, be theirs; we can all be miners, sailors, mountaineers in our play and in our forms of dress.

Dress in sport has enhanced the rituals which civilise potentially aggressive behaviour. A competitive sports conflict has the possibility of real conflict. The ritual behaviour between each team, and between both teams and the officials, and between the teams and the crowds are all delicate balances. These forms of behaviour have evolved over the century in which modern sport has developed. Rugby teams line up and clap each other off; the post-game social is traditional. Soccer teams, even the most professional and after the most severe 'fight', shake hands; the goalkeepers making a special point of the gesture. Basketball and volleyball have unique forms of grouping and cheering. In judo the rituals are an integral part of the bout.

In golf etiquette is often more important than the rules; nothing is more irritating to the experienced golfer than the player who does not know when to give way. The tennis player is astonished if a competitor wants to converse during the change-over. Correct behaviour in sport is essential for overall control of the situation; it is a vital element in making sport a force for social goodwill rather than one for antisocial violence. Many countries still look to us to be models of behaviour to the world; fairplay and sportsmanship were British qualities and British words which passed into the vocabulary — and practice — of world sport. Correct dress was not just a middle-class quirk. It was a means of showing respect for the game; respect for the opposition; respect for oneself. Have we not gone backwards in many of these departments? Cricket players now hug each other with the gay abandon of soccer teams and even seem to revel in the defeat and discomfiture of their opponents — the very essence of bad sportsmanship. One used not to leap in the air if one had bowled or caught a man out. Has the television camera something to do with this? Was the old-time British habit of biting the bottom lip and stiffening the upper lip, the masking of emotion, just a needless inhibition — or was it a valuable form of behaviour which rubbed off on to the spectators? When I see winning runners saluting the crowds with extravagant displays of affection and arrogance, I squirm.

Wasn't the passion for fairplay — the abhorrence of cheating — just the quality which eliminated any possibility of drugs invading sports practice? Isn't a return to this high-quality sports education the only ultimate solution to the drug problem? A true sportsman aware of sport as health, as a means of personal growth and development, as symbolic interaction between peoples and nations — would find drug-taking anathema. Any practice which interfered with the basic genetic balance of the human organism would be viewed with great seriousness — not flippantly and technically as some sort of training aid.

The difficulties which women still face in achieving full emancipation in sport are partly linked to ritual behaviour. Some of the reasons advanced for limiting women to certain sports activities are astonishing. It was not many years ago that I read articles by eminent psychologists stating that kicking was not in woman's true nature! Unmarried psychologists undoubtedly. It is interesting to consider in what ways women might invade traditionally male sports in the future. There are no valid reasons why women do not pole-vault and throw the hammer in athletics. Both events are more graceful and less strenuous than shot-putting. Women with the gymnastic ability evident in the asymmetrical bars find pole-vaulting easy and enjoyable. They also find satisfaction in the techniques of hammer-throwing, which use the whole body in a rhythmic and balanced way. A lighter hammer is needed, of course. Women are already playing football. The best women in swimming and track and field are better than good men. When women have been allowed to train with men and according to the same principles, their performances have soared; this is one of the reasons for success in East Germany. Mixed events are traditional in tennis; they are growing in golf. I can see no reason why mixed relays should not be commonplace in swimming and athletics. Basketball and volleyball are transformed and given a more sensitive quality, yet still realistic, when played by mixed teams.

Does the evidence suggest that we will see new games in the future? When games were exported they underwent changes: football developed differently in Australia, America and Ireland. There is rugby for thirteen-a-side and for fifteen-a-side. The major games are now all undergoing changes in size. The minigame is rife: minitennis in various forms; five-a-side soccer; seven-a-side rugby; junior hockey; eight-a-side cricket. The net to provide safety for circus performers became the 'trampoline'; trampolining is now a world sport. Acrobatics is now invading traditional gymnastics. The gymnastic beam became a springboard and then a stage; where can it go now? The modern gymnast has made miraculous use of his kinaesthetic sense, and his eyes, ears and touch to accomplish new skills. Will we see new combinations of apparatus to match the new skills? Will we see three asymmetric bars; four rings, two horizontal bars? combinations of these?

Rounders evolved into baseball and softball. Will there be new striking games? Will four touches become common in volleyball — or five? Will tennis be improved by not allowing the net-rush until after the third touch? Will the growth of masters' (veterans') sports be more carefully structured so that all sports have age range championships? Will we have 'handicaps' at more games, on the golf model, so that competitive sport becomes more meaningful at all levels. Where computer ranking in tennis is practised, the game seems more democratic; in the United States anyone, it seems, can creep up the computer rankings. Not so in Britain where it appears that subjective assessment still reigns. Three years ago I telephoned the British Universities Sports Federation to nominate a student of mine for the tennis trials relevant to the World Student Games in Sofia. I was told that there were no trials; the best players, men and women, were already known; both were studying and playing in the United States! I could not believe that a cardinal principle of competitive sport was ignored — put your racket where your mouth is!

There is only one way to demonstrate superiority in sport — on the field of play in open rivalry. Similarly the assumption by the new idols of the track that they can ignore country, district and national championships in pursuit of Olympic medals amazes me. The Piries, the Bannisters, the Brashers, the Disleys of athletics ran the full gauntlet of qualification. The Americans, to avoid suggestions of racial selection, still do, and any athlete with the spirit of the real champion can take all this in his stride. Let us make a quick return to the principle of qualification through competition — at events *designated* as international trials. Departures from this sacred principle are fraught with danger. Selection in athletics, for example, based on excellent *times* is not truly relevant for the Olympics and similar events. Here the winners are those who thrive in the cut and thrust of man against man running.

The history of soccer is also a fertile field in which possible new directions can be considered. Will teams remain eleven-a-side in the major game? Isn't the 10-metre rule common for free kicks in rugby, imminent in soccer? The offside rule has changed in soccer; it will change again. Two substitutes are allowed now; there was uproar when this was first suggested for British soccer not so long ago. The techniques of possession play ubiquitous in soccer today were copied from basketball; will the use of substitutes for each player become a *vital part* of tactical play in future soccer? Handling of the ball is allowed to goalkeepers; others can handle at the throw-in. Why not allow the single arm throw or throw-ins and introduce a new and attractive element into the game?

Will other variations of ball handling come (back) into soccer?

All this is on the assumption that the world of the future will find sport acceptable. There are already some philosophers of the Far Left who dispute this (see J.M. Brohm, *Sport: a prison of measured time*, London: Ink Links, 1978). They are anti-Olympic, anti-sport; to them sport is another tool used by the bourgeois, by the bankers, by the bureaucrats, by the party leaders to dominate and stifle 'the people'. Sports as we know them should be 'changed beyond recognition or abolished'. I find some of these arguments interesting and thought-provoking. I accept the point that modern sports administrators are heavily weighted in favour of aristocrats and royalty, bankers, generals — with white skins. I recognise that there is an almost total absence of electricians, trades union leaders, and editors of left-wing political journals; that politics in international sport usually means left-wing politics. But although I know what the far left is *against*, I am left in almost total ignorance of what they are *for*. I do not believe that a spontaneous revolution will sweep away social phenomena which have been part of man's social organisation since the beginning of recorded civilisation — and sport has been one of these phenomena.

I maintain the hope that there *will* be a place for sport in the future of the world. It will not necessarily have a place automatically or by accident. Left in the hands of unthinking and unfeeling exploiters — of both the commercial and the political kind — it could earn for itself an early death.

7

MAJOR ISSUES IN SPORT TODAY

I want to write initially in a human, rather than an academic way, about the major issues confronting British sport today. First I must reinforce my concern about the plight of physical education in the schools. Physical education, it must be repeated, is the cradle of the whole sports movement. There is no evidence that the true place of physical education in education is understood by those who make the ultimate decisions regarding curricula. I am not satisfied that the modern graduate teachers will 'live their subject' like some of the excellent 'unqualified' persons who enthused me — men who could do handstands and display other gymnastic skills past the age of sixty-five — an inspiration to all. It is also true that many, resting on their mesomorphic oars and extolling the 'you can be like me' philosophy, offended and even humiliated the thin, the fat and the clumsy children — alienating them for life.

I see no evidence that children today have as much time devoted to their bodies as I received at secondary school. How many enjoy three forty-five minute periods of physical training a week plus two long sessions at games? Inter-school games no longer seem to be appreciated for their potential value. In what other way do schools meet each other *en masse*? Inter-school games are unique as a way of teaching groups of children how to relate to other groups. Such relationships can only be taught by full utilisation of the rituals of sport: grace in defeat and victory; the ceremonies of correct dress; sportsmanlike behaviour at all times; the ritual handshaking, cheer-forms, applause. Are these fully understood today by the teachers and the children? It is physical education which can lay the seeds of sport for all; which can create a lifetime's hunger for movement; which can motivate the potential champion towards the search for excellence; which can educate the senses fully; it is sport as the major part of physical education which can develop the will and character of children. It is physical education which teaches the understanding of a skill well done and which provides the customers for the competitive sports clubs and federations — and for the 'sport for all' movement.

'Sport for All', this re-vamp of Coubertin's early cry of 'Every sport for everyone', is now common in most countries. Like 'Education for All' it can never be an actuality until government, both local and national, invests massively in plant and staff. The slogan is a good one, but the results do not yet affect the mass of the population. A serious research study by Political and Economic Planning (*Fair Play for All*, Broadsheet No. 571, Vol. XLIII) with the participation of the Sports Council showed that the larger sports facilities were used widely only by those who had the use of a car or lived within walking distance.

I have worked for twenty years at a delightful College in South East London. We have seven all-weather tennis courts; but because tennis no longer much taught in the schools, students arrive at college with little background in the sport. The 'tennis club' does not get off the ground as it once did, and there is little demand for regular use of the courts from the student body. There could be much greater involvement with the local community, particularly in the long vacation, when the courts are closed or used minimally; the same is true of the three gymnasia and the dance studio. The College itself stands in an ocean of industrial and public sports grounds and parklands. These, again, are not used intensively in the spirit extolled by the whole spectrum of mainline political opinion. Not far away there stands an athletics track of high standard; it has, among other things, an eight-lane straight. In the immediate vicinity there is an enormous concrete estate housing thousands of families, mostly young. The track is not floodlit, and it is invariably locked. Government after government makes the same plea for facilities to be used to the full, but nothing happens — why not?

There is one change which *could* transform the situation — the creation of a national recreation and sports coaching profession. 'A stadium without a teacher is dead,' said Carl Diem. The facilities I mention could certainly not be merely abandoned to youth and adult groups without supervision. This supervision should also not be casual and unstructured. We need a branch of the physical education profession which specialises in leisure-time recreation leadership and sports coaching. The time is ripe for the creation of such a service. We have among us many excellent young people trained as teachers at great expense, and unemployed. There are many teachers of physical education in this group. Better surely that they should be enabled to work constructively for the community than accept social security payments — as, of course, many do? Moreover, such opportunities would truly satisfy many young physical education teachers who gain inadequate satisfaction working in the 'generalised' curriculum of the schools.

We would also be better placed to bring to fruition the calls for 'dual and joint' use of facilities if we revolutionised the pattern of our school day. I was once the colleague of a great Norwegian hammer-thrower; he was an engineer who started work at 7 a.m., had a short mid-morning break, and completed his labours about 2 p.m. After a meal and a rest he could then train daily for two or three hours. This still left him the evening free for his domestic life and alternative leisure-time pursuits. Our own traditional school day — and working day, for that matter — is fragmented by unnecessary breaks. Why the lunch hour? Most people eat only out of habit or social 'duty'. If you get interested in tennis or squash you will be surprised how such energetic activities can be more satisfying than food! A school day starting at 8 a.m. and ending at 1 p.m., followed by a second 'shift' from 1.30 to 6.30 p.m. and a third shift for adult classes from 7 to 12 midnight, would ensure a better use of facilities. Cleaning would take place early in the morning or very late at night. Much as I believe in trade unionism, the caretaker should *not* have the power to dictate in such matters.

It is strange that there has never been any serious attempt to bring sports into the places where millions of our people live — blocks of flats and housing estates — or into the places where they work. Lip-service only is paid to such possibilities. I remember seeing the plan for a new housing estate near Munich where the *first* constructions were a swimming pool and an opera house; it became immediately desirable to live in such an estate. Imaginative schemes like this have been rare in Britain. The squash court complex and swimming pool in Dolphin Square, Westminster, is one example which was years ahead of its time. The enterprise of the Holborn Borough Council over the Oasis Swimming Pool was another. I remember swimming at the old open-air pool near Cambridge Circus and my sadness when a company asked to 'develop' a high rise block of offices. The local authority and the company eventually agreed on a novel plan: the lease for the land over 99 years would be reduced on condition that the company absorbed into their building — an outdoor swimming pool and sunbathing area, an indoor swimming pool and gymnasium, a sauna complex and a restaurant. This the company did very well. Why did this not become the model throughout the country? Is it lack of vision or mere idleness?

The provision for sport and recreation by industry leaves much to be desired. One can find outposts of excellence like the B.P. sports complex in South London and the Bournville complex in Birmingham, but the general scene is depressing. Employers and trade union leaders have been sluggish in exploiting the vast potential. Industrial sports facilities are usually designed for competitive teams; they are far from the place of work, and they are inadequately staffed. Compare the lot of the young person who elects to enter higher education. The university or college he attends will normally possess a sports hall, possibly a swimming pool, and, one hopes, tennis and squash courts. It will certainly have access to playing fields; the larger ones will have an athletics track. There will be a Director of Physical Education or Recreation supported by a full-time qualified staff with others coming in part-time. Transport to matches will be subsidised. Sports clothing will also be subsidised and there will be attractive meal prices within the institution. The student will have a chance to be Chairman, Secretary and Captain of a club; he can be member, player or supporter. Moreover there will be provision *within working time*, as well as structured possibilities in his leisure time, for him to train and compete. For the play- and recreation-minded there will also be abundant opportunities. This is excellent and I applaud it, being one who has always enjoyed such an environment. But if it is right for 'intellectual workers' it must be right for everyone else. I imagine one of the justifications is that 'intellectual output' is enhanced by participation in regular, healthful exercise. I am sure that similar provision for factory workers, bank clerks and all other workers would enhance the quality of their lives, improve industrial relations and improve production. Going to work should be a happy experience — just like going to university. If you want to see such a service in action, visit the headquarters of Marks and Spencers in Baker Street, London, where an exercise and health studio and sauna suite are supported by a medical team and resident osteopath. Although this is admittedly only provided for the executives, it is still a model worth copying for all.

The subject of medical provision for sport brings to light another grave weakness in our 'system'. I know of few international sportsmen who have managed to continue in top-level sport without recourse to osteopathic attention at some time. The fact that the current Captain of English rugby and an ex-Captain of English soccer were both 'saved' for sport by an eminent osteopath (Terry Moule, who successfully treated Gerry Francis and Roger Uttley) seems to be lost on the barons of the orthodox medical profession. Sports medicine and physiotherapy are hard to come by too. Unless he is lucky enough to befriend the trainer at a nearby professional soccer club, or live near one of the few 'athletes' clinics' in the national health scheme, the injured athlete can find his sports career in ruins.

There is another very basic problem — transport for competitions. I have worked in an honorary capacity for British volleyball since its birth, and have seen the sport develop into a flourishing association capable of organising, in 1978, an international tournament for sixteen countries of Western Europe. Because of increased Sports Council aid, it has been possible to staff the headquarters of the association adequately and to enter international competition. International players must, however, still invest large sums of money if they are to train, travel and compete properly; the sums involved must disqualify poor players from selection. At national league level there is little or no aid to the top teams. Local sponsorship is beginning, but it is neither massive nor regular. How can a student, for example, afford to compete in a national league which might require travel throughout the British Isles? How indeed can anyone?

Financing sport is a critical factor everywhere. If we wait for sports to 'pay for themselves' we will wait a long time. Some never will, but they are part of the international family of sports, they are socially valuable, they help to provide a full diet of sports for the young and hungry. If the cry to make soccer clubs fully multi-sport (and possibly multi-activity, multi-culture) were truly heeded, this problem would be overcome easily. In Spain, Real Madrid's basketball team is as well known as its soccer team. In many other countries, the soccer section patronises and 'mothers' the other sports, and is helped by other flourishing sports. Like basketball, to 'sponsor' the weaker brethren. In this way there can be a balanced development of sports across the board. Our own political parties have seen the light and pointed the finger in the right direction — taxation. By judicious changes in company taxation, income tax and rating regulations the professional soccer clubs could be brought to heel. If these clubs accepted their social responsibilities there could be an immense revolution in British sport — without recourse to more stringent financial measures.

There is a further simple financial measure which could be taken — social ownership of the football pools. The profits from these are enormous. Some countries, Finland and Italy for example, finance much of their sports programmes from football pool profits. In Finland and other countries where the climate limits the home league programme the pools are based on the English Football League for much of the year! If this is too much for free enterprise stomachs, we could merely halve the prizes and raise astonishing sums of money for the national sports programme. Take a look at the 'dividends' published in any week by the Pools Promoters' Association. You will find that a single prize of £600,000, and more, might be offered; this can be won by *one* lucky person — who I imagine would be more than delighted with

£300,000. Consider what could be built with £300,000: a sports hall and swimming pool complex for a community, together with many job opportunities. So in one year we could add twenty-six new sports complexes to the national resource and bring happiness to millions of people from 50 per cent of one maximum weekly dividend. This area of disgusting greed is one that is not highlighted and attacked by the Sports Council — and not enough by the politicians, perhaps for fear of losing votes. Similarly with the equally degrading buying and selling of players. In 1978 it was assessed that a total sum in the order of £12 million changed hands in the *two months* before the end of the tax year. This explosion was due, of course, to tax laws which prevent clubs adding to their facilities (considered unfit for allowance against tax) but allow them to purchase players as necessary industrial input. Be that as it may — and what a tragedy that it is so — we have to decide as a society between individual greed and community need. My own mind has been firmly made up for many years. Sport is a social service, every bit as essential to human health and happiness as education and medicine. By such tactical adaptations of the present system, without added taxation at national or local level, we could rapidly transform the structure of British sport.

The Hurlingham Club in London is an exclusive multi-sport club; it offers tennis, squash, swimming and indoor games, besides dances and club dining and wining facilities. It could easily offer more games, as it once did. Such a model was 'exported' in the last hundred years to many countries. If you visit Buenos Aires, Cairo, Bangkok and many other capitals in the world you will most likely discover a palatial 'sports club' built on this principle. The only region not following this example seems to be the regions of the British Isles outside London! It is the same with 'training camps'. These excellent devices for helping talented sports persons to reach the full flower of their talent were condemned, twenty years ago, as copies of East European models. In fact they were copied from what for more than a century enabled countless Oxford and Cambridge rowing teams to reach their peak. Once these Oxbridge privileges were to be extended to 'the masses', it was as if some terrible sacrilege was being committed.

8

WHAT THE POLITICIANS SAY

Because of the massive investment which the modern state makes in facilities and personnel for sport, I thought it would be interesting to test the current thinking on sport of the political parties in Britain. This I accordingly did in January 1979.

The Information Officer of the Liberal Party wrote expressing regret, saying 'We do not have a published brief on the subject.' The Conservative Central Office sent a copy of the speech by Hector Monro, then the Opposition spokesman on sport, and this speech represents the current authoritative Tory position on the matter. In his preamble Monro blames the plight of British sport in financial terms on mismanagement by the then Labour government. He calls for a number of palliatives, e.g. rate relief when a club makes its facilities available for the general public, the replacement of grants by low-interest loans repayable out of revenue from the facilities provided, and dual use of schools facilities. There is also some firming-up of the Conservatives' philosophy regarding sport. It is no longer seen as a luxury, but rather 'a growing part of the everyday life of the great majority of British people, of all ages'. It is 'important for the mental and physical health of the nation' for us to recognise now the vital contribution that can be made by recreation. This particular statement establishes that all political opinion, at the official level, in this country recognises the relationship of sport to public health. Concern is shown for the disabled, and for the gifted in sport: these gifted athletes should be provided with time for better training and access to it, and 'a supply of money permitting the athlete to continue to develop his or her talents for the nation's benefit'. Both public and private investment in recreation is called for; private corporation sponsorship would be increased if the taxation system encouraged such investment. Not only should the big tournaments with the prestige prizes be helped; money spent on incentives for young athletes, on facilities for small local sports clubs, and towards efficient management of sports governing bodies are 'every bit as worthwhile'. The role of sport in the struggle against vandalism gets strong support, and the importance of intensified aid to inner city areas is stressed. The Conservative statement concludes with a call for progress: sport is at a threshold; it can stagnate or move forward, with forward momentum depending on two ingredients — leadership and financial resources.

The Labour Party referred to a background paper, entitled Sport and Recreation, prepared for a working group at their twentieth local government conference at Cardiff in 1976, in which they remark that their last policy statement was in a paper entitled *Leisure for Living*, published more than fifteen years earlier. Its author was concerned that although there had been publications on broadcasting and the media, and on the arts, other forms of leisure had been totally neglected 'even in such comprehensive policy statements as Labour's Programme 1973'. Nevertheless credit is given to Labour's achievements in government: their role in the establishment of the position of Minister for Sport (now Minister for Sport and Recreation), their work for the consolidation of the Sports Council and Regional Sports Councils, the relevant Countryside Act of 1968, and finally the publication of the 'White Paper on Sport and Leisure'. The inhibiting effect on intentions for sport of the 'present economic difficulties' is recognised. The paper thus addresses itself to the problem of how best local authorities may ensure that 'the limited resources available to them for recreation are employed with discrimination and in the most cost-effective way possible' — in accordance with 'socialist priorities'. Attention is drawn to the increasing development of a 'corporate approach' to recreation illustrated by the growth of local authority Recreation and Leisure Departments. The Labour thinkers also justify their concern by reference to the role sport might play in combating vandalism and in contributing to personal health and mental wellbeing. They specifically relate this to 'unquantifiable economic savings in terms of time lost at work, inefficiency, etc.' They ask again for a better use of existing facilities, for sensible staffing arrangements which would make this possible, and for management arrangements which would bring the users into the management process, e.g. the governing body of a sports centre including representatives of the using organisations and individuals. It might have its own budget and be free to 'manage' as it thought fit. Like the Conservatives they ask that appropriate rating relief be given where voluntary clubs make their facilities more generally of use to the community.

The Labour Party also referred to their 1976 Programme where many of the points raised in the Cardiff paper were reinforced. Community facilities run by the community itself would save money and create a greater sense of belonging. Facilities owned by the armed forces, industry, and the schools should be made available for public use; also race courses. High charges should not work against use; there should be acceleration in action for 'recreation priority areas' in inner city districts, and sports excellence should be encouraged by an expansion of the Sports Aid programme. (The establishment of the Sports Aid Foundation* and an increased effort by the British Olympic Association regarding Olympic training funds have given some reality to these hopes.) It is recognised that an improvement in Britain's international sporting performance would help to stimulate fresh interest and demand for all kinds of sporting activities. There is also a renewed plea for better access to the countryside: most particularly, public footpaths should be protected, and we should be keenly alert to encroachment on public access to water and mountains by private ownership. The Briton's access to public footpaths is an ancient and possibly a unique heritage.

It is appropriate to mention here that at its annual conference in 1979, the Trades Union Congress sponsored a welcome initiative by issuing a rare major statement on sport. This coincided with the establishment of a TUC Committee for Arts, Sport, and Entertainment and with the fact that the TUC Education Committee was asked to join with the CCPR Youth Committee to advise the British Olympic Association on selection for the forty-strong British youth contingent at the International Youth Camp for 1,500 young people accompanying the Moscow Olympic Games. The TUC statement commented on the low general level of participation in sports in Britain; it is lowest in the working class, declines with age, and is more male than female; it is worst in inner-city areas. It called for special efforts to be made for the most deprived groups in society — inner-city dwellers, ethnic minority groups, the disabled and the unemployed. The TUC called for better use of facilities, systematic skills teaching, improved accessibility of centres, and the involvement of the local community in planning and management.

The 'Young Socialists' have also pronounced on sport. In their 'Charter for Young Workers' they call for a massive increase in sports and cultural facilities; they ask that the schools be available

*The Sports Aid Foundation was established in 1976 by the Minister for Sport and Recreation, Denis Howell, and the Sports Council. It has an independent governing body and exists to help the leading performers in sports. It was patterned on the West German 'Sporthilfe' organisation. The Foundation raises its money in a variety of ways including a pop concert by Elton John, a lottery, and through collections in pubs. Grants from the SAF enable leading athletes to take time from work for training and competition without loss of earnings. The Director, Alan Weeks, is quoted as saying 'We think we have a reasonable compromise between the college system in the States and the State support of European countries.'

more fully in the evenings and holidays so that sports facilities 'do not lie idle for three months of the year'. They demand that 'the businessman and profiteering' be 'kicked out of sport'. Football — an industry — should be nationalised and put under the control of the trade unions and the supporters' organisations.

The Communist Party has updated aspects of its original policy statement issued nearly two decades ago, which, however, remains essentially valid. The new statement (*Leisure and Recreation in Britain Today*, by Terry Bushell, 1975) is not a definitive policy document but 'a contribution from our Party and the Young Communist League to the discussion on this question now going on in many cultural and sporting organisations of our country as well as in the Labour and progressive movement'. The statement provides interesting insights on the history and philosophy of leisure as seen from a Marxist standpoint. There is a precise analysis of the administrative structure of the Sports Council and its relationships with local authorities; the plea for better facilities of all kinds is reinforced. Clear answers were given to a questionnaire distributed to political parties by the CCPR prior to the 1974 (October) election. The Party suggested that real advance is impossible without a proper network of facilities starting in the schools, these also to be available to school-leavers and post-school organisations. Sports equipment should be available free at school: children not happy with a diet of the dominant sports (football, rugby, hockey, cricket and netball) should have an alternative. A five-year plan for facilities was proposed: a 'Crystal Palace'-type centre should be built for all communities with over 50,000 people; competent, well-paid instructors should be available; all towns with over 20,000 people should have a swimming pool, an athletics track, tennis, football and cricket facilities, and other sports amenities. All housing estates should include playgrounds, swimming pools, gymnasia, etc. A figure of £300,000,000 was suggested for investment in this sports development plan, to be provided by the government — a sum equal, the authors pointed out, to four weeks' expenditure on arms. The statement places recreation and leisure on a par, and concludes with the thought: 'As mental and physical health are closely related, the neglect of one leads to the deterioration of the other, and as the maintenance of both depends largely on leisure activities, it is to be hoped that working people look seriously at the provision of goods and services necessary to such activities.'

From a sports point of view, the manifestos issued by the British political parties in the 1979 General Election were hardly inspiring. The Conservatives, in a policy statement of thirty-two pages, found room for only one sentence: 'Sport and recreation have also been hit by inflation and high taxation. We will continue to support the Sports Councils in the encouragement of recreation and international sporting achievement.' The Labour Party, in forty pages, scored no better. Their sentence read: 'In a society where leisure is increasing year by year, Labour wants to make facilities for sport and leisure available to all. We will continue to put more money into these activities.' I could find no mention of sport and recreation in the Liberal manifesto; nor was there even a specific mention in the programme of the Ecology Party — a pity because there seems to be a good argument that sport, recreation and conservation are inter-connected. In the only National Front document I saw (pushed through my front door) there was no mention of sport — not surprisingly, since the logical result of the 'send them back now' argument would be the immediate depletion of the Britons of Caribbean origin who form about 60 per cent of our national athletics team and are beginning to make their mark at soccer, basketball and volleyball! The Scottish National Party found more room that most. It said: 'The S.N.P. proposes an increase in the status and powers of the Scottish Council for Physical Recreation. The Council should be representative of the sporting and recreational clubs and associations of Scotland, with two main responsibilities to the Government. One would be to advise on the state and needs of Scotland as far as sport and recreation are concerned. The second duty would be the administration of government funds for training, coaching and other facilities. The encouragement and development of these should be undertaken on a community basis wherever possible. The Council should also be responsible for organising Scotland's participation in international sporting events.' The SNP also pronounces on an Anglers' Trust which would ensure good water management and better relations between anglers and farmers, and it calls for the encouragement of mountaineering, hiking and camping for Scots and visitors with special attention to the needs of youth in open-air activities. The Communist Party was thin on sport: it saw sports associations as part of a general army of cultural and professional groups, struggling together 'for better health, housing, education and other services our people need'.

Was the situation, I wondered, any better across the Channel? Before the French parliamentary elections in 1978, the journal *Education Physique et Sport* asked the four principal French political parties to express their opinions on the subject of the future of physical education and sport in France. The parties concerned were the Republican Party (P.R.), the Communist Party

(P.C.F.), the Socialist Party (P.S.), together with the United Republican Party (R.P.R.) and the Party of Reformers, Centrists and Social Democrats (R.C.D.S.). A summary of this opinion survey appeared in the Warsaw periodical *International Review of Sport Sociology* (Vol. 4, 13, 1978), in English. The questions posed to the parties were searching. They were asked to define the guiding principles of their sports policy and their attitudes towards the training of physical education specialists at all levels of education; the role of the sports governing bodies in training personnel; sports facilities, planning and financing; the proportion of emphases regarding sports for all and competitive sport; the preparation of French national teams for international competition; the development of research; and an evaluation of government structure which would ensure the optimum development of sport and physical education policies.

For the Republican Party the present formula for the organisation of sport in France is 'a lucky marriage between the state structure and the sports associations'. It should be maintained with certain amendments, such as entrusting one ministry only with responsibilities for sport. The Party felt also that the state had a responsibility to improve the position of France in international sport—with regard both to the 1980 Olympics and the more distant future. The image of a nation, rightly or wrongly, is judged by its international performance in sport, and once a decision to take part is made, there should be serious approaches to participation. The Republican Party saw three distinct categories of sport: first, sport for all—recreation and entertainment for pleasure, without serious competitions; secondly, sport competition—mass sport organised in clubs providing a 'proper basis for competitive sport'; and thirdly, sport for top-class competitors—requiring a special 'mode of life' involving self-denial, effort and limitations on the development of one's career. It was considered necessary to work out plans for the careers of champions and 'guarantees for a professional future'. Republicans wanted improved specialisation among physical education teachers in primary, secondary and higher education. Sport is a social fact, it is a need, an 'inevitable necessity', and a 'condition for survival'. Sport helps people 'irrespective of age' to maintain equilibrium and to adapt to modern life. It is 'one of the indispensable elements of a happy life'. The Party also called for exercise breaks in work places and for the protection of the moral value of sport (by fighting such dangers as violence and the 'drive to get money').

The French Communist Party thought that any possibilities for improvement in sport were 'inseparably connected with the entire transformation of society'. Each human being, it claimed, should have free access 'to the achievements of physical culture', and it was the duty of the state to ensure that these aspirations became facts. There should be a vast increase in state aid to sport; the number of specialist physical education teachers should be substantially increased and they should all have completed higher education. The Party was of the opinion that central, rather than local, government should have the major responsibility for the building and maintenance of sports facilities. Both mass and competitive sport deserved help. Sport was an important component of the quality of life; the 'existence of the individual cannot be limited to the satisfaction of elementary needs'. A champion, by improving his skills in sport and his own character, 'creates a sports spectacle which can contain cultural worth', and in so doing serves as a model and stimulus for the masses. At the international level sport, just like any technical, scientific or cultural form of co-operation, is a factor promoting international understanding and peaceful co-existence. It is 'the common language of mankind'. For such reasons purposeful steps should be taken to raise the level of national teams, to improve discovery methods in the area of sports talent, to improve research techniques and communication, and to 'regulate the status of the competitor as a representative of his country'.

The Communist Party was critical of the prevailing state administration of sport in France; it was 'developing features of encroachment and is almost smothering'. They also advocate one Ministry to be responsible for all matters concerning sports, but suggest the establishment of a 'Higher Council of Physical Activity and Sport' made up of 'representatives of the state administration, social and sport institutions, as well as teachers, parents and pupils'.

In the programme of the Socialist Party, preference is given to the development of school sport and sports associations; the educational value of sport and its potential as a factor in building democracy are emphasised. The Socialists are in favour of mass sport, seeing it as 'cultural emancipation of the citizens'. In order to achieve it the 'state should accept its obligations' concerning the training of physical education teachers and other sports specialists. The national teams should not be pampered, neither should they be ignored. Sport should be treated in such a way that every French athlete should 'have the right and be given the means to go in for competitive sport'. If this improved the results of national teams in international competitions, it certainly would be a good thing, but it 'should not be an aim in itself'. Similarly with regard to research in sport: this should be conducted on a large scale, embracing medical and psychological examinations, but it should not focus on narrow and purely practical objectives, such as 'better results'. In general, the Socialists in France think that physical culture means the right of every citizen to practise sport on a level that is in accordance with his skill. They also recognise that the development of sport depends not only on sports policies, but also on the 'evolution of society and social transformations'.

The group of Reformists, Centrists and Social Democrats saw sport as part of an overall strategy for education, entertainment and culture. It was 'a condition of the country's health'. Financial assistance should be more to the clubs and less to the federations; the clubs that accepted older people, the disabled and children of school age should have preferential treatment. With regard to the national teams, 'there can no more be any place for dilettantes, since the competitors of other representative teams devote eight hours daily to training'. The United Republican Party asked that athletes representing the nation should be helped during their period of activity *and* given special aid to 'facilitate their return to socio-professional life' after the completion of their sport career. A 'career plan' should be suggested to each champion; proper training would be assured; there would be medical care; an ordered 'life style' would then be 'a guarantee of moral peace and a future'. The Social Democrats also postulated that the national teams needed a status which would protect them from the predatory forces of both private interests and political forces, and which would also save them from 'the hypocrisy of a pseudo-amateur status', permitting them to practise 'their art' without worry about their future professional prospects.

The Polish author of this study, Wiktor Lisowicz, assesses these policies briefly. The sport policy of the Republicans he sees as mainly 'instrumental', a means to various ends: sport is to make society more healthy, decrease the number of accidents at work, raise the prestige of France in the international community, and so on. They are dissatisfied with France's present sports situation but they do not 'supply a deepened analysis of the reasons for such a state of affairs'. They do not see any revolutionary changes and 'limit their programme to proposals or amendments, modifications and improvements'. Much of their plan would involve only a small privileged group; they give the impression 'that it is their intention to achieve a marked improvement with the help of the most modest means possible'. Lisowicz sees the sharpest disagreement between 'left' and 'right' in France as being about the financial aspects of sports development. The 'right' generally saw a financial input from the three main factors — the state, the municipal authorities and the 'social associations'. The size of the state's share was an open question. The 'left' felt that the state should accept the major burden. The group of 'centre' parties thought that a drift of capital from richer to poorer branches of sport could be arranged by manipulation of the tax policies and by low-interest loans.

In the United States too politicians have been preoccupied with organised sport. This had been brought to a head by the poor showing of United States teams in Olympic Games, in comparison with the Soviet Union. For many years there has been strife between the AAU (Amateur Athletic Union) and the NCAA (National Collegiate Athletic Association). The latter purported to be the national 'umbrella body' for sports, and thereby achieved recognition by international sports governing bodies. The NCAA represented the higher education sector in American sport, controlling the majority of the athletes and the major sports centres. In an attempt to bring an objective voice to the dispute, a 'President's Commission' was established. This was composed of Congressmen and leading ex-sportsmen and women, of whom perhaps Willye Whyte, Bill Toomey, Ralph Metcalfe and Rafer Johnson are the best known, supported by a team of twenty-five researchers, analysts, consultants and secretaries. This powerful team set out to determine what factors impeded the United States from fielding its best teams in international competition.

Their report (*Final Report of the President's Commission on Olympic Sports 1975-1977*, US Government Printer, 1977) is of great value to students of sport. They found that few countries relied so heavily on the educational system for the development of amateur sport as did the United States. This educational system, they agreed, was the envy of a large part of the world, and it had served the United States well as a proving ground for world-class athletes in certain sports. But, even in educational institutions, funds were growing scarce. The pressure on individual athletes to begin earning a living and raise a family precipitated many early retirements from American sport. However, they noted the positive factors: the national characteristics of individualism, perseverance and *esprit de corps*, which had resulted in outstanding performances by American athletes since the very beginning of international competitive sport. The unique aspects of the system were 'the fount of her strength, as well as the source of her weakness'. Many of the factors inhibiting international participation were self-generated, the team claimed, and could be traced to a lack of organisation and inadequate funding.

Their major recommendation was thus the creation of a Central Sports Organisation (CSO) to resolve the organisational conflicts and fragmentation which plague the American sports system. The organisational framework for the 'Moon race' is offered as a model for sports administration, with 'imaginative marshalling of resources and a fine combination of skill and courage'. The American sports population was seen as isolated within a large, passive society in which 50 million people never exercise and in which degenerative diseases associated with obesity and physical inactivity have reached the epidemic stage. They likened American sport to the state of the nation after the Revolution: 'a loose alliance of quarreling states ... bristling with sovereignty or absorbed in their own concerns'. The solution was 'a structure of government which lay between the tyranny of the King and the chaos of independent states'.

The Commission called for five major reforms:

1. a means to settle organisational disputes over the right to be the recognised national governing body in a sport;
2. a means to induce all organisations with significant national programmes in a sport to belong to this recognised national body so that their activities could be co-ordinated;
3. a means to guarantee an athlete's right to compete;
4. a means to finance amateur sports more effectively; and
5. a central policy-making forum to identify American sports problems and to effect solutions.

In 1978 the Senate approved legislation co-ordinating all amateur sport under the United States Olympic Committee. The Bill included a proposal that $30 million should be earmarked for the USOC programmes. A central Olympic Training Centre has been created at Colorado Springs.

Political attitudes to sport in the socialist countries are becoming extremely well documented (see J. Riordan (ed.), *Sport under Communism*, London: C. Hurst, 1978). Suffice it to say, for the purposes of this discussion, that in these countries sport has achieved a status equal to art and science. The state plays a major role in the training of specialist teachers and coaches, and strenuous effort is put into research activities, the results of which are actively disseminated. The problem of 'amateurism' has been solved, since every sportsman has another profession or is absorbed into the sports movement after his competitive days are finished, as organiser or coach. In recent years there have been some interesting compromises with ideological principle; in tennis the 'socialist amateurs' play against the 'professionals' in the top open tournaments, but much of their prize-money may be paid into the coffers of the national tennis federation. In the 1979 Spartakiade and, it seems, in the 1980 Olympics there will be every facility for the advertisers, the commercial entrepreneurs and the soft drink manufacturers to flourish. It will be interesting to see if such compromises will destroy the central 'purity' of the sports movement in the socialist countries, which has often been the secret envy of many Westerners who study their sports programmes and policies. This is not to say that those countries advocate 'sport for sport's sake'. The socialists are often quite frank about the role they see for sport in society. A recent resolution of the DTSB (Deutsche Turn- und Sportbund) of the German Democratic Republic makes this quite clear. It reads: 'The IXth Congress of the Socialist Unity Party of Germany set the tasks for us all. By further shaping advanced socialist society in the GDR, we are creating the fundamental conditions for the gradual transition to Communism. This is an historical process of thoroughgoing political, economic, social, intellectual and cultural changes marked by the socialist way of life at work, during free time, in the work collective, and in the family. Better conditions for the comprehensive development of the individual within the collective are permanently created. Physical culture and sport play a great part in this. Regular sport promotes health, recreation and physical fitness'. The DTSB are justly proud of the advances they have made on all sports fronts, and chart their objectives as 'attracting more people to physical culture and sport; continuously developing children's and youth sport; developing especially the Spartakiade movement; encouraging free-time sport and regular practice, training and competition, and promoting sports talent and the striving for top class performances'.

A most frank explanation of the East European analysis of the amateur/professional dichotomy appeared in the *International Review of Sport Sociology* in 1977 (Vol. 3[12]). The author, Barbara Krawczyk, drew attention to statements by top United States politicians accepting that the state should help potential champions to reach full fruition, and reminded us that Coubertin, as early as 1905, expressed scepticism over attempts to codify the status of amateur athletes: 'Amateur sport is not a set of rules but an opinion, something like a mood. It could not be imprisoned in a cage of narrow-minded formulae'. Despite attempts to codify amateurism and eliminate sports which seemed more 'professional' than others, and the successful elimination of the Olympic art competitions, there has — the author explains — been increasing state, academic, and industrial patronage for sports. Krawczyk also argues that the ancient Games were not so selfless as some would have us believe; the idealists often ignore the knowledge that benefits (e.g. pensions allowances) could accrue to the winners of the Olympics in classical times — and their families. The ideology of amateur sport, she says, 'has its roots in the contradictions between work and play so typical of class societies'. There then follows an explanation of the ambivalent attitude towards the growing 'professionalisation' of amateur sport; on the one hand, some try to defend traditional attitudes, which would 'retain the features of sport which reserve it for the privileged only, as a component of a style of life free from the necessity to work'; on the other, there is the cry, made clear by Coubertin in 1919 when he said 'On whose order are the broad masses of people to remain outside the Olympic movement?'. The Olympic idea can only be fully realised as a 'result of the full democratisation of social life, as one of the consequences of the socialist social system'. At the moment sport is in a difficult situation; 'it should not lose its properties of play, but it simultaneously accepts some features of work ... ' In the socialist system a top-class athlete enjoys social privileges, has free time at his disposal for training, has the guarantee of good material conditions, a coach and equipment which is free of charge. An athlete is granted such privileges 'not only to enjoy pleasant experiences but also to supply such experiences to the community he represents through his behaviour and attitude. In addition to the chance he has been given to develop his talent, he has the chances for promotion, fame and social recognition.' This harmonious combination of the contrasting elements of work and play 'transforms sport into difficult but exciting kinds of creative work, full of self-denial and creative asceticism'. There is the constant effort to go beyond one's limits and to search for the improvement of the human being. This transformation of sport from selfless play to an activity which has the features of useful work and is socially important does not thus 'signify the degradation of sport competition'. Just the opposite — it 'gives sport a new symbolic meaning and value'.

To conclude our survey of political opinion and attitude I ask you to identify the national sources of the following quotations, in which some key-words have been altered so as to conceal their origins.

1. 'The physical well-being of the nation is an important foundation for the vigour and vitality of all the activities of the nation; failure to encourage physical development and prowess will undermine our capacity for thought, for work, and for the use

of those skills vital to an expanding and complex society.'

2. 'Our sports are a vanguard force in the Revolution, and their function is a means of entertainment and cultural participation by the people. The role of sport is not economic but educational and recreational. Sport and physical education are an integral part of the development of the socio-economic and political structure, serving public health, education, and social integration.'

3. 'Sports are a valued means of building up the country. For us sports are not an amusement but an absolute necessity for the strengthening of our people.'

4. 'Physical culture plays an integral part in the political and cultural training, and education of, the masses.'

5. 'Physical Education can help in the task of creating a hardier, more vigorous, better poised and happier people and must therefore occupy a prominent place in the national programme.'

6. 'Participation in sports develops the characteristics of a socially responsible personality, viz. responsibility, courage, fighting spirit, willpower, self control, friendship, self-discipline, devotion to moral ideas, and the proper relationship of the individual to the group. One of our great humanist aims is the recruitment of the whole nation to physical culture and sport. This is seen as an extension, a restatement in the modern world, of Coubertin's claims that "the vigour of the citizens today creates the vigour of the state tomorrow".'

While sociologists, psychologists and other experts may disagree profoundly about the fundamental purposes of sports, there seems to be much unanimity of opinion among the world's politicians. (*Key*: 1. The United States (John F. Kennedy); 2. Cuba; 3. China; 4. The Soviet Union; 5. Zambia; 6. German Democratic Republic.)

9

SEVENFOLD AGENDA

In the summer of 1979 we were all forced by Prince Philip, in his capacity as President of the Central Council of Physical Recreation, to face up to the problems of sports administration and control. He criticised the role of the Sports Council in British sport, and complained about governmental influence nationally and internationally. He called for a Royal Commission to investigate British sport so that scarce financial resources might be better used for the benefit of sport by streamlining the organisation. The Chairman of the Sports Council sprang to the defence of his organisation. Sports writers and sports officials took sides.

There is general agreement in the country that the matters raised by Prince Philip in his articles and his speeches (to the 'Fellows' of the Physical Education Association) are worthy of serious attention. There might not be one easy model which we can copy, but we can certainly do better than we are doing. The problems are complicated. We do not live in a society which has a written constitution. We live in a mixed economy. We do not have one official political philosophy to underline our thinking; we do not even have one religious outlook as a people. Most of us, most of the time, have to make compromises. This should not be our excuse for not trying to improve our systems of social organisation — including the organisation of sport. Can we put these complicated problems into a manageable framework for more precise analysis? I think we can, and I propose to discuss the following major issues which need urgent solutions in Britain: an ideology for sport; leadership for sport at all levels; facilities; programmes; research and information; administration; and finance.

Our first big problem, an *ideology* for sport, is a big one and involves short-term thinking about long-term questions. We have to ask ourselves — what sort of society do we want and what role should sport play in that society?

'Sport' can be many things. We can see it as a means of public health; as a part of a balanced education; as a form of theatre; as a means of international understanding and celebration of national cultures; as work; as commerce; as a means of national development; as an expression of national identity; as a forum for social and symbolic interaction; as war without weapons; as art; as adventure and challenge; as an area for social mobility; as fun. Without an ideology we cannot frame objectives; without objectives we cannot evaluate progress. Our ideology is our argument: the argument which persuades governments to spend substantial amounts of public money on sport and physical education. Without an ideology we are at a loss to analyse situations which involve an overlap in the functions of sport. We need to get our priorities right. Until we do this we will be thrown awry in the sports-political field; we will misunderstand the unity of sport and thus allow a single sport to offset all the good done by a multi-sport movement like the Olympics. We will find the amateur/professional problem unnecessarily complicated (we might reflect on our acceptance of the need for full-time professionalism in soccer when Malmö, a team of part-timers, can meet Nottingham Forest in the European Cup). We will allow a minority group to deny millions the full possibilities of a full day of leisure (Sunday). We will always be thinking off the top of our heads; our arguments will be mere rhetoric.

An ideology can be created best by outstanding people. So *leadership* is the second factor. On the one hand we cannot surrender sport to an aristocracy; on the other we cannot surrender it to a dull bureaucracy. Both the voluntary and the government sectors must be respected. Final decisions should be made jointly. We need excellent administrators, excellent coaches, excellent physical education teachers. There should be no conflict between 'excellence' and 'mass': this argument is a red herring. Sport-for-all and championship sport are the two ends of the same spectrum, and good leaders understand this.

Leaders should be imaginative and innovative; they should work in community recreation and coaching as well as in schools, sports associations and clubs. They will invent new forms of participation and competition and they will have the capacity to motivate people. Leaders, at all levels, breathe life into sport. They breathe life into *facilities*. In many ways we have excellent facilities in Britain. It is their utilisation which is tragic. The community is often deprived of facilities for which it pays through rates and taxes. Throughout the country schools and colleges deny easy access to them. Professional soccer clubs, and other sports, restrict public use of their facilities. Even at community sports hall level there is a 'throughput mentality' which sees the participant almost as a statistic. Sports halls, to become clubs, must be run by the people who use them. Unless the people who use these centres labour on them physically — painting, cleaning, organising, protecting — the solidarity of a true 'club' cannot be achieved. In the giant brick and mortar deserts of our cities we allow urban developments which are an insult to physical man; no living complex should be allowed which does not provide amply for swimming and other health sports.

Facilities are determined by *programmes*. Once we have determined our needs ideologically, we can establish objectives—and devise programmes which will enable us to reach those objectives. We need to decide how much of our unique games culture we want to protect and enhance; how much of the world family of sports we need to import. We need programmes designed to cater for talent and for playful leisure, for the Olympic programmes, for the handicapped.

Such programmes need to be permanently monitored. Therefore we need efficient *research and information* systems. Sports medicine needs urgent treatment. Sports statistics should provide us with instant knowledge of how many facilities, leaders, competitions, and so on, we have at a given moment. Predictive research should be able to advise us on future needs in twenty, fifty, even two hundred years. It is to be hoped that the media will collaborate responsibly. There were examples of horribly irresponsible reporting at the time of Montreal. The East German girls won gold medals galore, which was not received with enthusiasm by many British reporters, who used phrases like 'fish farming'. Pictures emphasised muscular development, and there were suggestions that the champion ladies were biologically not truly feminine, and so on. When a year or two later the United States girls, making use largely of the training methods of the German girls, and displaying the same muscles which are essential for good swimming technique and performance, won gold medals at the World Swimming Championships, there were no such scurrilous suggestions. The many sports writers who regularly present fair and objective comment were certainly as ashamed of these lapses by colleagues as I was.

In order to motivate and educate a whole society in sport, committed sports writers are needed to help people make choices and decisions. If I had my way, 'professional wrestling' would no longer be treated as part of 'sport'; a rational debate would be conducted on the relationship between sport and tobacco sponsorship; sports-political questions and other controversial problems would always be discussed at as sophisticated a level as possible and with all possible objectivity and awareness of the wider context. The Chinese have always had a point about the Taiwan issue and this should not be obscured; the South African issue should not be blurred by being linked to 'political' issues elsewhere. Israel is not beyond reproach and the Palestinian view on sports representation should be heard. There *is* doubt about the value of boxing as a sport, and people should not be made to feel afraid to say this; the professional foul in soccer is *always* wrong; thuggery in rugby is *always* wrong; referees should *not* be pilloried by television play-back. The 'drug' problem would be treated in the context of cheating and of interference with the basic metabolic processes of the body—not in the hysterical manner of Fleet Street. Sports writers have a big responsibility in these matters—and they have a lot to answer for. We need 'think tanks' in which sports planners, sports writers and physical educationists take a serious and humanitarian view of things.

Sports *administration* is the problem of the moment. It is impossible to compel complete administrative tidiness in an area of free choice like sport. I would ask for one thing immediately—that when we in the world of sport relate to the outside world we do not quarrel. Internally I think that the right administration would evolve if we had the right ideology, exciting and pertinent objectives, and programmes with a good chance of reaching those objectives. Administrators, backed by teams of highly motivated leaders at all levels, would work collectively towards shared objectives. The right administrative machinery would then develop. In a sense even the present infighting between organisations is not unduly worrying—unless it becomes squalid and involves the sabotage of the initiatives of others. That people *want* to become involved in sports administration is a credit to the sports movement itself. The voluntary sector attracts to itself an enormous amount of brainpower—often not available to professional sports administration. Take, for example, the brainpower in the British Olympic Association—senior lawyers, engineers, doctors, educationists and businessmen, who would not find life rewarding as full-time sports administrators. Sport needs such highly-qualified volunteers; sports administration, like sport itself, should also be 'for all'.

But part-timers cannot handle the whole of the sports movement. Government, both local and national, must have its voice. The sport machine needs the back-up of professional sports officers who work throughout the country. The Minister for Sport and Recreation must have an opinion which should be received responsibly by the community of sport. The major problem seems to be—who should have the final say regarding leadership? In our society it would seem that a body which is *elected* must have that ultimate responsibility. I have a further thought: the voluntary sector in sports administration is staffed by people who usually have one foot in active sport and the other under the administrative desk.

This, I suggest, ought to be the pattern for the professional sports administrator. To have both feet under the desk, from 9 to 5, five days a week, is not the best lifestyle for the sports administrator. One solution would be to insist that one full day a week for all Sports Council employees should be on attachment to clubs, recreation centres and fitness groups. There is nothing better for a sports administrator than to wear a track suit for some of the time.

The critical problem underlying all this is, of course, *finance*. If, ideologically, we conclude that sport is an integral part of society — at the same level of priority as art, science, health and education — the theoretical side of the problem is solved: we *must* divert adequate national resources to fund the sports movement. Such funds would not undermine the concurrent need for sport to continue developing its own financial resources — fees, gate money, lotteries, selective patronage and other enterprises — but it would mean that the sports movement was not subject totally to the hazards of this tenuous system. If, on the other hand, we insist on the easy rhetoric of 'sport for sport's sake', sport will go on looking for handouts, degrading its spirit and its message. It seems to me that there is a connection between using sport as a billboard without restriction, *via* sport conducted without observation of a strict code of fairplay, to violence on the terraces. If sport were upgraded in priority, if it became recognised as equal in status to education — it would not be faced with such problems as that concerning tobacco sponsorship. Few would suggest that education should be the plaything of a commercial company for advertisement purposes. Few would agree that because the initial letters of Canterbury Cathedral are the same as those of a famous soft drink, it should be fair game for advertising. Why are so many seemingly unconcerned when sport is asked to prostitute itself? And all so unnecessary when the vast football pools profits are milked from the sports movement, when the taxation system prevents even those football clubs with a social conscience from ploughing back their proceeds into multi-sport facilities, and when the television companies exploit the magic of competitive sport events at fees well below their proper market value. Sport itself generates tens of millions of pounds; too little goes back to water the roots. This must be changed.

There are no easy answers to the problems of organising sport in society today. There is no one model which can be copied and immediately internationalised. Each country must search for answers which suit its cultural patterns, its history and its aspirations. However there can be two answers for optimists: they can try to predict how sport *should* evolve in a world permeated by ethical principles and civilised behaviour; and they can design sports programmes which, bearing the long-term hopes in mind, reach acceptable compromises with the world as it is. In the search for these positive answers they can come to understand how sport might degenerate if abandoned to mere market forces as a commodity to be bought and sold, or if exploited and prostituted by other forces. Alternatively they can come to realise how frequently, and at how many points, sport touches 'real' life, and how central it is to the hope for mankind's future sanity.

10

HOW OTHERS ARE DOING IT

I have been extremely fortunate both by accident and design in my sporting travels over the last thirty years, and I want first to dig into my memory for some impressions concerning the manner in which others handle the problems in sport enumerated in the last chapter. For, let it be said, the problems are ubiquitous. No country has yet found the perfect answer to 'administration' in sport — how to balance the state and voluntary forces involved.

My first overseas experience of sport was in Cyprus; I spent a year there from 1949 to 1950, before the term 'developing country' had been invented. Greeks and Turks lived happily together. I was impressed by the organisation of the Famagusta 'Gymnasion' or the secondary school, its curriculum based on the mind-body-soul triad of antiquity. I saw so many lessons in athletics that I still remember the Greek for 'On your marks, get set, go!' It was here that I became acquainted with volleyball and made the first transitions from sprinter to hammer-thrower. I attended the annual ritual 'Dance of the Flowers'; I saw village football matches; I played three-goals-and-in on Famagusta beach. I was suddenly aware of a culture in which sport had a real and significant, day-by-day involvement. It was a rich life for a sportslover — topped off by a swim in the Mediterranean, and grapes, goat's cheese, rye bread, Commandaria wine and Turkish coffee in a beach café at night. My love of travel and sport, together, was cemented then. Since that time I have made international and comparative sports studies central to my career and life. I became aware, in Cyprus, that sport could be more than soccer, rugger and cricket with a sports day thrown in — the typical British boy's sports diet at that time.

I have always tried to maintain a truly global outlook on sports problems. It came as a surprise to find early in my career that sport and politics were indeed linked at times. There were some village soccer teams in Cyprus frowned upon for their allegiance to the trade union movement 'Akel'. There was the time a few years later when a Belgian policeman asked me to leave the plane I was taking *en route* to throw the hammer in the World Student Games in Berlin in 1951; to be fair he was acting as proxy for the then

British Home Secretary, Herbert Morrison, who had taken the overall decision to interfere with the Berlin Games. I realised that left-wing politics in sport *were* politics whereas right-wing politics were not!

I have made two short visits to Canada. The first was to Vancouver for the 1954 Commonwealth Games, and I was struck by the enormous potential of the country for recreation — and the little that was being made of it. In 1976 I returned to Montreal for the Olympic Games and witnessed then what a carrot like the 'Games' can do for a nation's morale in sport, its organisational ability and its across-the-board sports development. I saw how a 'Western' country could make successful selective adaptations to 'Eastern' selection, training and coaching methods. In Australia, for the 1956 Olympic Games, I was on the fringe of the first discussions concerning Unesco's involvement in sport, and was aghast to see the athletics track at Melbourne Cricket Ground being taken up only hours after the end of the last event. Melbourne must be the only Olympic City to have profited so little in terms of permanent athletics facilities. I came across Percy Cerutty* for the first time and was reminded of the need for sport to be ever ready to embrace the eccentric and the 'non-regular' into its family; we have, lately, become far too concerned in our field with diplomas and qualifications. Australia interested me also in its carefree attitude to work. An ambitious athlete at that time would think nothing of working as a milkman so as to order his training day better; there was no snobbery regarding job status.

In Scandinavia I lived at the Bosön Sports School and studied at the Gymnastic Central Institute. I also taught English at Bosön and privately in the city of Stockholm, and felt I caught the atmosphere of the place. I first saw orienteering practised as a 'sport for all' phenomenon. I wallowed in the excellence of Bosön, that fine sports centre on the Baltic — still one of the most beautiful in the world — and was there at the time when a letter arrived from Stanley Rous, then Chairman of the Central Council of Physical Recreation. Stanley wanted to know all about Bosön because the London County Council were intending to develop the Crystal

*Percy Cerutty began running in middle life, but became one of the greatest coaches of modern times counting among his protégés the famous Herb Elliot. An out of work Australian, he once contemplated suicide; but looking at the horses racing in Melbourne, he was suddenly taken by the beauty of their movement. His whole life was transformed. He became a student of movement, exercise, the body, body-mind relationships, and especially athletics. Not only was he a mentor to many young Australians but he practised what he preached. Until advanced years he was still in good physical fettle.

Palace site! Again, as in Cyprus, here was a society in which sport was central to life with abundant facilities, good job opportunities, and a judicious mixture of championship sport and mass sport. Handball was also at its beginning as a major international and Olympic sport.

In Finland I experienced the harshness of a Northern winter and learned how marvellous *langlauf* skiing can be; I came to understand the lure of the sauna; and saw how facilities can be community-owned and community-protected. Finland is the one place where I know I can see sports facilities without graffiti. I will always remember the Finnish Olympic Stadium where the 'tower' is an attraction for tourists — both national and international; its height exactly equals the distance thrown by a prewar Finnish javelin champion. The revenue from tickets for the lift to the top pays for much of the upkeep of the stadium! Among the facilities one finds a museum of sport and a sports medical clinic. The stadium also houses sports administrators, youth club headquarters and other sports facilities. This and most other sports facilities in Finland are paid for from profits of the state football pools which, ironically, are often based on the English football league games. In Finland one is again struck by the sports-political influences. The 'workers' sports movement (TUL), the 'national' sports organisation (SVUL), the sports association of Swedish-speaking Finns — these three have their own sports centres and federations. The third of these springs from a history of colonialisation; the first-named caused by the expulsion of 'reds' from the 'white' sports organisation after the 1917 revolution in Finland had failed. All so fascinating for a naive Englishman brought up to believe in sport for sport's sake!

In Finland I was always astonished at the adaptability of the sports movement to the climate; the hundreds of athletics tracks converted in an afternoon to ice hockey and bandy rinks — by the use of a hosepipe. Illuminated ski paths through the forests; the whole family going off on skis to see Grandma on a Sunday afternoon. Saturday is sauna day, the women and children going first — and returning to cook supper; then the men; followed by a whole-family canasta session at night. I treasure the memory of a packed audience at Olympic wrestling in Helsinki; 10,000 people educated to understand true wrestling as physical chess — unbelieving of those who think 'professional wrestling' to be either sport or realistic. I think too of a magnificent character called Robert Oxe, lent by Finland to Sweden as national wrestling coach; an early example of a sports common market.

The Swedish Royal Gymnastic Central Institute is another

unique Nordic development. Built by the city authorities, it is adjacent to the Olympic Stadium in Stockholm, and its facilities are, by statute, to be available daily to the sports clubs of the city. This means that the 'students' must be away by 5 p.m. nightly; thereafter until almost midnight the city clubs make use of the place. The GCI, as it is known, was one of the first institutes to develop exercise physiology as a science — and relate it closely to championship sport and sport for all. It was also very early into applied psychology for the same reasons. Moreover, the traditional link between physical education teaching and physiotherapy (a link developed by Per Henrik Ling) has not been entirely lost. No Briton can visit the GCI, built in memory of Ling, without thinking of Madame Osterberg — a graduate of an earlier GCI — who made such an impact on physical education in British schools. The oldest College of Physical Education in Britain — hers — which was built at Hampstead, but is now at Dartford in Kent, still bears her name — even if now in parentheses!

I arrived at the Sporthochschule in Cologne late one night in 1952 with nothing but a haversack and £60. I lived for one semester in a type of Nissen hut, sharing a room with seven German students at a cost of £1 a month. Coffee and tea were still in short supply. I found it possible to work hard, train hard and lead a healthy life on bread and milk for breakfast, soup for lunch and one main meal a day. The Sporthochschule had been re-established in 1947 by Jack Dixon, a British army physical educationist. Jack brought Professor Carl Diem, who had organised the 1936 Olympics, and his wife and a few other teachers from Berlin — from the old High School of Physical Education at Charlottenburg — to the community-owned stadium and sports complex in Cologne. There in simple facilities they recreated a German sports study tradition. At the same time, of course, in East Germany the Leipzig Sporthochschule was also being established. Thirty years later, in 1977, Jack Dixon, by then retired, was awarded an honorary doctorate by the Cologne Sporthochschule. Even at the time of my stay in 1952 the facilities in the Müngersdorf Park — in which the Sporthoschschule lay — were impressive. The main stadium was surrounded by swimming pools, cycling areas, hockey pitches, free play areas and gymnasia — all owned and maintained by the city of Cologne. Nearby was a special assembly point in memory of 'Father Jahn', the founder of 'German gymnastics', where once a year a torchlight procession and ceremony is held to honour the memory of this German who also struggled for the realisation of a pan-German state in the last century, and in so doing used 'sport' as a means to achieve national identity. I have visited the

Sporthochschule many times since, most recently in 1978, and its development surpasses the imagination. Its sports science department is the envy of the 'West' — and many of the same teachers who were working there in the early post-war days are still practising. Better facilities do not in themselves do anything for the quality of teaching, but a good teacher will work well in a farmyard. One Sporthochschule teacher I remember well is the gymnast Helmut Banz. He was a prisoner-of-war in England at the time of the build-up for the 1948 Olympic Games in London, to which the Germans were not invited. He was released ahead of time to help coach the British gymnasts (several of whom were of course connected with the Army Physical Training Corps). Another notable teacher was Professor Ernst Jokl, a refugee from Hitler who had worked in South Africa for many years, and had just returned to Cologne. It was this particular mixture of people and the climate of 'rebuilding' — materially and emotionally — which made the Sporthochschule so absorbing.

I treasure one other impression from my studies in Germany. In 1957 I was a member of the British athletics team which lived at Baarsinghausen, the Sports Centre near Hanover. This was one of many sports centres built in the regions with profits from the German football pools. The same old story! Its director was a graduate of the Cologne Sporthochschule. There was one outstanding piece of enterprise at Baarsinghausen; a commercial inn/hotel connected with the sports centre; the proceeds from this inn were used to offset the costs to sports people living in. Tourists and others were happy to utilise the abundant sports facilities available and to pay the normal prices for accommodation. I have been talking about, and writing about, such matters ever since — but to little avail.

No visitor to Roman sport can miss the great building of the Italian National Olympic Committee (CONI). This is the powerhouse of Italian sport. It involves more than just the Olympic sports; it covers sports science, sports medicine, sports planning; it employs more than 2,000 people. It controls the distribution of profits from the Italian football pools industry. Need one say more? The Rome Olympic Stadium recaptures the spirit of antiquity; in a complex which includes not only magnificent sports facilities of all kinds but also the National College of Music, it is used to the greatest extent possible by the National School of Sport. I always have the feeling that people are *welcomed* into the precincts of the Rome stadium. You see women with prams and old people just resting. I shudder when I try to pass some of the uniformed gate-keepers at our stadia whose main mission seems to be to park cars as far from the main building as possible!

The Netherlands and Belgium are not countries noted for their international sports successes, but they *are* interesting in terms of ideas. For many years the Dutch have been experimenting with new ways of running sports halls; how to make sports centres into sports clubs. Among the ideas generated in the Netherlands have been those whereby committees representing the users have been given a budget by the local council — and then made responsible for its sensible use. The sports and physical education centre at Leuven University in Belgium is also worth a visit from anyone interested to see how such a complex can be small, beautiful and productive of very high-level work. Liège University boasts a similar centre.

Apart from a fleeting visit to San Francisco and New York, *en route* from Australia to London, after the 1956 Olympics, I missed out the United States for a long time. Having been brought up on American text books in physical education theory and physiology, I thought I knew the people and the system well enough. I also had the rather cynical attitude of many British educationists towards anything American. My first real visit, in 1974, showed me that I was wrong. I was invited to contribute to a three-week summer school at Long Beach University, California. The campus was part of the State University system, and the summer school was designed for teachers and others interested in questions concerning international sport and physical education. Courses took place every evening from 6 p.m. to 10 p.m. This assured maximum attendance since many students wished to take up summer jobs in day-time. Courses were all recognised for higher degree accreditation. The students were of very high calibre and so demanding in their seminar work that I felt exhausted after a week.

The campus was delightful, with every possible facility including the most modern jacouzzi (whirlpool) baths. The facilities were utilised in a very democratic way by the local population, who could merely 'attend' and play tennis or racket ball, or swim — or practise golf and athletics. There appeared no special privileges for staff and students outside working hours. For the handicapped there were specially tailored programmes in sports. Elite squads were also catered for, as were 'deprived' youth groups from downtown Los Angeles. For a small fee visitors could check out a tennis racket, plimsolls, shorts and a shirt; the university laundry maintained a ready supply of such hire equipment. One of my strongest memories of Long Beach is of 'stretch ball', a game which symbolises the American capacity for imagination and innovation. Children in primary schools are asked to bring one wire clothes hanger (the type available in any cleaners), some elastoplast, and an old hose stocking. The hanger is bent into a diamond shape and the hose stretched over this frame. The remaining hose is then wound round the handle of the hanger and squeezed tight with the elastoplast. This provides an excellent 'bat' for hitting a ping pong ball. At a stroke, a bat and ball are provided for every child at almost no cost, and all the racket games can be practised sensibly. My other memory is of the intelligent by-law which compels oil companies exploiting the wells near the coast to plough back a major percentage of their royalties into recreational facilities — within a specified distance from the coast. This accounts for the enormous number of golf courses (often among the oil pumps), swimming pools and marinas in this part of the world.

In the 1950s Britain seemed to have endless athletics matches against Poland, Hungary and Czechoslovakia, and I came to know these countries quite well. In Hungary I knew particularly well the Director of the National Stadium, Imre Nemeth, who won the gold medal for hammer throwing in the London Olympics of 1948. He was appointed Director of the Hungarian National Stadium on certain conditions, one of which was that he should *concurrently* follow a course in physical education at the National Institute of Physical Education in Budapest. This was typical of East European enterprise in higher education in sport — and was copied by Cuba and other countries that follow this line of study. The feature is that there should always be both regular entry to higher education, and *irregular* entry. This latter is to accommodate those who enter late in life, and those whose early education was disturbed in some way, the late developer, the talented sportsman who needs more time to develop his intellectual potential, and so on. 'Irregular' courses are also designed using correspondence and part-time study techniques. These courses might stretch to seven or eight years, but the final diplomas are of the same standard as those offered to 'regular' students, and job opportunities are the same for both. From Czechoslovakia I am left with a major memory; the development of physical development research centres for children. Even in the early 1950s these were well staffed by research workers and sports medical specialists. Obese children received special help.

It occurred to me then, as it does still, that we know far too little about the effect of exercise on children — and adults. How do specialised programmes compare with generalised programmes? Would a specialised programme of only swimming give good overall physical results? Would it compare with a programme based entirely on gymnastics — or soccer — or any other single activity? How much time is necessary to achieve meaningful results? Are two or three thirty-five-minute periods of general physical education in schools anything more than lip-service? As we get older do we need more or less exercise? Which activities are advisable and which are inadvisable? In Czech and other East European research institutes for sport they have been busy on serious research of this kind for more than thirty years, and today we are witnessing the results. In Czechoslovakia, Poland and Hungary there was also a fine tradition in sports and physical education dating from before the Second World War on which to build. Hungary had one of the best trained and equipped teams in all the early Olympic Games and used to export coaches (Otto Szymiczek went to Greece to be national athletics coach there in the 1930s, and is there still). The Czechs, of course, had developed the *Sokol* movement to a very high level many years ago. Like the *Turnvereine* it was a sports movement with direct nationalistic overtones, but it was a 'Pan Slav' and not only a national movement. The slogan 'every Czech a *sokol* [a falcon]' was the slogan of a people striving for national identity under the imperial rule of Austria-Hungary—just as 'every German a *Turner* [a gymnast]' was a similar striving of Germans under the domination of Napoleon.

It was a Pole who conducted the first serious international comparative study on sport and physical education for a world government organisation. This was Dr. Eugeniusz Piacecki who, in 1928, made a study of thirteen European countries on behalf of the League of Nations Health Committee. The Warsaw Academy is a powerful hothouse for sports developments. The Sports Research Institute on the same campus provides scientific back-up in physiology, psychology, sociology and general sports theory. In it more than 100 researchers are engaged full-time, including a numerous group of translators: not surprisingly, I have often found these people better read than myself, even in the English language. This Academy (AWF) was early into practical learning technologies; high jumpers listening to amplified sounds of their own approach and take-off foot pattern; gymnasts learning from a video screen which depicted the exact relationship of each of their body components to the others. 'Autogenic methods' (self-hypnosis) for relaxation training have been employed ubiquitously in Polish sport for very many years; such 'switching off' techniques are as important as 'switching on' methods in sport. In Poland one notices an abundance of general and specialised sports newspapers. These are aided by state organisations; there is so much in sport which *must* be published — but which is not commercially viable.

The AWF also possesses a first-class Olympic Centre. This is a hostel for the national élite squads and a hotel for visiting teams.

The concept of 'special treatment' for such squads grew up after the Second World War. With food short and utter devastation around (let us not forget that Warsaw was 98 per cent destroyed by the Nazis), the people still hungered for sports success. Sports success builds morale; morale is the ingredient for sparking off national recovery programmes. Talented sportsmen were thus allotted extra rations and privileged training conditions, and in return they were made to feel a social obligation — a sporting patriotism. This general philosophy still pervades Polish sport. It is a philosophy manifested in the astonishing network of 'Polish Olympic Clubs' abroad. Wherever there are Polish *émigrés*, you will find a 'Polish Olympic Club'.* These clubs organise dinners and other events to raise money for the national Olympic teams. In some — Canada and the United States, for example — they raise enormous sums of money. Clubs 'adopt' members of the teams and invite them to speak at events. Every two years there is a 'jamboree' in Poland for members of the clubs worldwide. This spirit is also manifested by the Polish National Stadium in Warsaw, which was built by voluntary labour in the years following the Second World War, literally from rubble. Students were all expected to give a number of hours each week to this mammoth task, and for sports and physical education students, it was not just an expectation but an obligation. It is this involvement in the actual physical labour of their creation which causes respect for sports facilities. Thirty years later, there is a tremendous sense of pride in the generation which built the stadium. And what a stadium. The approach is gently uphill — then a vast bowl unfolds, containing 100,000 seats: an architectural gem which has provided the model for stadia in many other parts of the world. I first saw this stadium in action at the time of the September *Dozynki* ('harvest festival'); here sports events, air displays and folklore are all combined to create a mass sports-ballet of great passion and beauty.

In Poland I first experienced a 'training camp'. Experience had shown that such a camp, for the national athletics team, should last no longer than sixteen days. For physical and psychological reasons this was the right length. Three such camps were held annually, the first before the season; the second before the national championships, and the third before the major international matches. Attendance was voluntary, and athletes could bring their families if they wished. Indeed at the camp I attended, the famous steeple-

*Cultural ties overcome political barriers: some Poles, totally opposed to the political complexion of the present government, still contribute to the Olympic fund. The British Olympic Association has started 'British Olympic Clubs' abroad on this pattern.

chaser Jerzy Chromik was one who elected not to come. The days were idyllic for sportspeople; two hours of hard training every morning and two very light and recreational hours every afternoon. Coaches and athletes worked out together; there were excellent sports medical facilities.

I discovered an interesting development in the area of tourism, of relevance here because of the administrative link that then existed in Poland between tourism and sport: the organisation 'Autostop', otherwise hitch-hiking. In Poland in the mid-1950s the ownership of private cars was not greatly developed and it was expensive for young people to move about the country. The government had worked out several ways of helping them to get to know the Polish territory; this was necessary since the 'new' Poland had lost land to the Soviet Union on one side and gained it from Germany on the other. This movement sideways meant a new orientation, and travel played a fundamental part in this process. Motorists were encouraged to give lifts to young Poles. Young people were thus asked to register for 'Autostop', which entailed depositing a small sum of money in a bank and registering for one week's community (voluntary) service every year. Such work could for example be for old people or on farms. Each traveller carried a book of stamps, which were given to the motorist in relation to the number of kilometres for which a lift was given; on the cover of this a vivid 'target' was displayed so that, when shown at the roadside, it would encourage passing motorists to stop — knowing that officially, at least, the applicant for a lift was 'honest'! Motorists clocking up the most 'lift stamps' would be awarded prizes by various sponsors of the scheme, including Polish Radio.

The idea that, due to its political system, Eastern Europe forms a monolithic 'bloc' is, of course, absurd. The similarities between the countries of Eastern Europe are, naturally, significant, but the differences are even more so. The suggestion that the Czechs should develop a network of Olympic Clubs is received by them as ingenuous: Czech émigrés have never shown the same love for their homeland which is so evident among Poles. There are historical conflicts between Poles and Czechs; at a pre-war tennis championship a well-known player did not appear owing to a territorial dispute between Poland and Czechoslovakia. Poles and Hungarians, on the other hand, have experienced an affinity in history, which sometimes shows itself in the applause which greets Hungarian sports teams in Poland and vice versa.

The Soviet Union is different again from them all. So much that is valuable has been written about the Soviet Union that I have no intention of writing much about it here. I have visited Moscow four times; once as an athlete, twice for seminars, and once as a member of a delegation of educationists. From a professional point of view I have always found my visits positive and have always learned something new. During my first visit, a few athletes were dragooned into visiting the great 'exhibition' centre in Moscow. We went out of politeness more than anything. But what a breathtaking educational experience it was; I had no idea what an 'exhibition' really meant. A few of us, teachers, also visited a Moscow secondary school, quite spontaneously as we were passing by. We were welcomed warmly and met our counterparts; one can learn so much from the corridor in any school — the report on the school camp, the number of sports clubs, the debating society, and so on. It has been my normal experience worldwide to find that teachers of physical education have similar objectives and similar personalities. The visit to this Moscow school confirmed my own prejudices! To compete in the Soviet Union (not merely Russia, I should add) is to meet spectators who are sophisticated in the field of sport. They recognise a good throw particularly — and a bad one. I remember this distinctly and will carry the sound of 60,000 whistling Russians to the end of my days. 'How can you get 60,000 people watching athletics?', I asked. 'Easy' was the reply. 'We arranged that an international soccer match between the Soviet Union and Czechoslovakia takes place one hour after the end of the athletics meeting; those who want the best seats must come early!'

On my most recent journey, in 1977, I was a member of a small group of physical educationists, including the Directors of Loughborough University Physical Education and Sports Sciences Department, and Carnegie College, Leeds Polytechnic. We had descended on Moscow as part of a Thomson Winter Tour. With no advance planning — since Moscow did not reply to our letters — we merely knocked at doors. The British Embassy could not believe the tale of successes we reported at the end of the week. At the Olympic Committee, the University Faculty of Physical Culture, the Lokomotiv Sports Club, the Lenin Stadium, the Dinamo Club, and on the ice rinks attached to the blocks of flats, we were received with invariable kindness. The lady Dean of Students at the University Faculty gave us almost a whole day of her time. The Director of Dinamo, the largest of the Soviet Union's 'sport societies', enthused over the commercial successes of his 'Society'. It seems that Dinamo now has more than twenty-eight industrial enterprises based on sports goods and sports equipment; the profits from these mean that the Society no longer relies on either trade union or state support. As on my first visit in 1959, I was struck by the utilisation of the Lenin Stadium; the numbers of young people *using* the stadium campus for sports of all kinds; the pensioners taking part in exercises under medical supervision; the families 'picknicking' in the grounds of the stadium. The gymnasia were available for the weightlifters and the wrestlers underneath the stands and there was an obviously high ratio of coaches to sportsmen. This ratio is perhaps the basis of Soviet sports success. In the Soviet Union, coaching *is* a profession. Yet many of their facilities would not pass our safety acts; most are merely adequate from the point of view of safety. But they do have enormous numbers of skilled teachers and trainers, and ultimately this is what matters. Investment in people is better than investment in sports property.

During this visit I also developed one or two worries. I noticed that the Soviet Union seemed bent on out-doing the capitalists concerning the relationship with sponsors in sport. The 1979 Spartakiade and the Games of 1980 involved a quite disproportionate amount of trafficking between sports officials and sponsors. I hope that the Soviet Union does not abandon its stance regarding sport — that like art and science, it should be a right and not a privilege for all — and certainly not subject to the whims of commerce, public relations experts and advertisement managers.

I worried also over the fragmentation and over-theorising about sport in the University Faculty of Physical Culture. I met a young woman who appeared to be the Head of the Department of Pistol Shooting in the Faculty of Firearms — or some such. It occurred to me that it might be slightly ridiculous if, for example, we built a Faculty of Cricket with a Chair of Spin Bowling. I worried at the excess of smoking among sports officials and the absence of any strong campaign to dissociate sport from the attempt by tobacco manufacturers to give social approval to the habit of smoking. I worried at the seemingly blanket approval given to the sport of boxing, with little thought to the arguments against the sport. I wondered how those with views contrary to agreed policy in sport might express them.

My first visit to East Germany was in 1951 to attend the World Student Games in Berlin. These occasioned much political heat since they were part of the World Youth Festival of that year. The political establishment in the 'West' had marked them down and did everything to prevent sportsmen attending. I had first heard of the Games through Duncan White, an Olympic athlete from Ceylon with whom I was very friendly at Loughborough College. Other factors encouraged me to attend, and to cut a long story short, I arrived on the day the athletics events at the Games ended. I was there long enough to hear, see and feel the atmosphere. It certainly was 'political' in the sense that people in the stadium were exhorted by slogans to work for peace, build the country, increase production, etc., and I was reminded of it during my second visit in 1977 for the 6th Spartakiade in Leipzig. Only in England, my host said, was sport expected to be totally non-political!

In 1951 the 'border' in Berlin was still a chalk mark on the pavement. In the eastern sector of the city some impressive stadia and swimming pools were already in evidence. In the succeeding years I have followed the growth of sport in East Germany with particular interest. I followed it in the years when the 'non-political' sports leaders of many countries acquiesced in the ostracism of East German athletes; and in the years of astonishing development when the East Germans said 'OK, we will use sport to force you to recognise us' even if in less simple terms. And force us they did — like the Cubans in response to the embargo placed on them by the Organisation of American States. I come back time and again to this political involvement in sport to reinforce the fact that it exists; it cannot be ignored; and it is surely not one-sided.

The Spartakiade of 1977 was a model of organisation, of excellence, of mass participation, and I have never seen so many fit and skilled young people. It is difficult to understand a sports culture which involves brass bands, marching and mass displays — when one has been reared in a culture which does not have these manifestations. In Germany sport has always been politicised, and always associated with nationalism. In most countries in the world this is so, which does not mean that it is always right, any more than it means that it is always wrong. This is something needing constant debate and thought in a rapidly changing world.

The astonishing sports success of the German Democratic Republic arouses endless guesswork. Cynics point to drugs and 'genetic control' — among many bizarre explanations. I feel the reasons are more simple. When the GDR was established, it had the chance to rebuild its sports and physical education system almost from scratch. There was no sports establishment to overcome; most of the administrators were young and many were trained in physical education. All were highly motivated politically, and the national youth movement was brought directly into the sports movement — and vice versa. With such basic factors in their favour, it should be no surprise, after thirty years of scientific planning, systematic training and graded competition, that their results — across the whole spectrum of sport — should be superb. There is one final factor: the GDR leaves much of its sports control in the hands of the DTSB (the Deutsche Turn- und Sportsbund), with the State Committee for Sport and Physical Culture playing a supporting role. The DTSB has a mass base and a powerful leadership. This leadership has chosen a selective programme for GDR sport, i.e. a programme which emphasises those sports in which the GDR might expect to shine internationally and especially in the greatest shop window of all, the Olympics.

In Romania much attention has been given to early selection and specialised training, within the schools physical education system. There are specialised secondary schools for sports where students receive twelve hours of 'PE' a week under highly qualified teachers and coaches; there are schools where there might be emphasis on one sport e.g. track and field; there are afternoon 'sports schools' organised both by the state and by leading sports clubs running junior sections. As in all these countries, there is a very active research institute with multilingual archive and translation systems — studying developments worldwide. Sports medicine is in abundance and free. Romanian doctors wishing to specialise in sports research and treatments must complete a one-year course in this area, after normal medical studies supplemented by a physical medicine course; they must also, concurrently, complete a 'trainers' course' in an appropriate sports discipline. They are then attached to one of the sports organisations and can work full-time in this field. One significant common factor in the East European 'systems' is the higher education of those interested in a sports career. Higher Institutes of Physical Culture train teachers *and* coaches. There is usually a common core programme for two years, after which students choose either general PE teaching or specific sports coaching. Teachers work in primary and secondary schools; the coaches work in the sports federations, in local government, in sports clubs, and in the holiday centres established by trade unions and factories. It must be remembered that trade unions in these countries pay careful attention to health, and 'spa treatment' is more readily available for more people than is common in the West. Sports writers and commentators often have a physical education background. There is no doubt that a sports qualification is sincerely respected by the public at large and by the academic world. The levels of ability required match those for medicine, and it is not unusual for PE people to move into medicine after their first or second year.

I have been particularly fortunate in my studies in the Third World.

This classification has already broken down with the acceptance of a 'Fourth World' of the 'least developed nations' and a totally new situation occasioned by the emergence of oil-rich nations, which have suddenly found themselves in possession of immense financial resources, but discovering quickly that some skills are not to be easily bought. Some of the countries have a good civil service but are weighed down by overpopulation; in others too much land is owned by too few people, or the military have total power, or there are rich indigenous cultures. Most are poor, diseased, illiterate, with high unemployment, and — not surprisingly — unstable. What is surprising is the great and ubiquitous popularity of sport. Whether the planners like it or not, people everywhere seem to love sport. In Juba in the Southern Sudan the only paved road, four years ago, led from the airport to the stadium. Despite enormous poverty, a match between Juba and a Khartoum soccer team attracted 10,000 people, paying £S1 each, to this stadium in 1978. However, the stadium in a developing country is also the marshalling yard for political and social (health, for example) campaigns of all kinds. Adjacent to the airport in Juba is a large field in which, traditionally, young people gather twice a week to dance and sing. Against this colourful backcloth of sound, colour and rhythm, the '707' makes a strange sight.

In 1971 the Pan American Games were held in Cali, Colombia. When I asked the Mayor what value this had for his community, he replied 'If you could have seen what the Games did for the morale of the people of this city, you would not ask that question.' The transportation, the post and telephonic systems, all the technical services associated with modern life received a boost. The people thought they could not do it; when they achieved success there was a profound collective pride. In order to house 6,000 athletes it was necessary to build special accommodation; this 'village' afterwards became a much-needed Polytechnic. In order to feed such large numbers, new technology was imported from Switzerland: a Swiss expert was persuaded to stay after the Games and give the Colombians the longer benefit of his experience. Around him and the gleaming kitchens had then been built the nucleus of one of Latin America's first school meals services. I could not understand why cycling was so popular in poor countries; cycles are an expensive item. It had not occurred to me then that cycling is the one sport which takes the sport *to* the villages. Every night there is an exciting end to the day's racing for possession of the 'yellow jersey'. In rural areas where villagers rarely go to town, let alone the cities, cycling comes *to* them. On the basis of this mass interest, governments can more easily collect taxes for road improvement! As René Maheu, late Director General of Unesco, once said, 'a country needs its stadia as it needs its airports; both are a symbol of modernity.'

The 8th Asian Games were held at Bangkok in 1978. They were a unique occasion. Not only were they supported by the local population with verve and passion; not only were the facilities those used for two previous Asian Games and close to the city centre; not only were these facilities used normally as the headquarters of Bangkok's youth and sport programme and a base for such social services as work to solve drug abuse; but it was the first time that a regional games had been paid for by those taking part. A consortium of Gulf states had guaranteed the basic administrative costs. This left the organisers to invent supplementary ways of increasing takings, such as sponsorship, television and radio fees, ticketage, and state grants. The whole thing approximately broke even and pointed the way to future developments. This was a more encouraging event than the African Games in Algiers, also held in 1978, or the Asian Games of Teheran held four years previously, in neither of which had there been the obvious involvement of the population in evidence at Bangkok; in fact there had been an ominous absence of spectators. It was indeed difficult logistically to reach these stadia — no buses, no underground railways — but the population also seemed 'unaware' of the Games, despite the magnificence of the stadia in Algiers and Teheran respectively. In Lagos, at the Second African Games of 1974, the Nigerians, once they were made aware of this, made excellent efforts to bus in the local children — free of charge. All countries must endeavour to maximise the effect of these major regional Games. They all supplement the Olympics in form and in spirit. If Olympism is truly practised — in its athletic and fine arts forms — such regional festivals are the best opportunity to supercharge the sports movement in the host-country.

In the Arab countries there are some interesting experiments in sports organisation. In most there are Ministries of Sport and Youth, and all borrow generously from whatever pattern of organisation in the world attracts them. There is no apparent ideological barrier to these influences. In Kuwait, for example, the Supreme Council for Sport is composed of the Prime Minister, the Ministers of Defence, Education, Social Affairs and the Interior, the President of the National Olympic Committee, and three persons elected from the sports movement — a high-powered group on the lines of some East European states. Kuwait has also taken a selective-sports path; ten sports have been chosen for emphasis. In each of these there are national squads at under-16, under-19, under-23 and full national level. Football gets special treatment. There is now a football school producing trainers; four Brazilian coaches support eight Kuwaitis in the national squads. Brazilian soccer techniques have been selected at national level in place of

British; the British style is considered too physical, and unsuitable for the hot climate of the Gulf. Each sport is nourished by the introduction of top coaches from countries where the sport is at a high level: the Soviet Union for volleyball, the United States for basketball and athletics; France for fencing, West Germany for swimming and handball; China for table tennis and gymnastics. Kuwait was also able to launch a completely new club structure a few years ago. Fourteen multi-sport clubs were created with teams in several sports, and leagues were able to start immediately. Needless to say, each club started with enviable facilities and coaches from abroad where necessary. At one time three of these clubs employed British soccer coaches. In Libya the Olympic complexes at Tripoli and Benghazi were also the result of multinational efforts; British architects, Bulgarian builders, French technicians for lighting and scoreboards. In Algeria the Olympic Stadium was the work of Brazilian, French and Hungarian designers. In Saudi Arabia there is a mushrooming of facilities — frightening in cost and complexity. Unfortunately there is a feeling in the Arab world of having been taken for a ride by overseas builders, 'experts' and exporters — out for a fast buck. The establishment of a powerful Pan Arab Sports Confederation — embracing all Ministries of Sport, all National Olympic Committees and all Arab members of international and regional sports bodies — should go a long way towards sorting out such problems. The first meeting of this body was at Rabat in May 1979.

When one studies the role of sport in the Third World the problems for all of us are brought into high relief. It is clearly impossible to make a strong case for sport if the 'list of priorities' method of analysis is used. Sport would come a long way down a list — starting with hunger and including disease and poverty. But this is not the way that people or systems work. Development seems to advance best on a broad front; growth and change are required *now*. Changes from pastoral-nomadic ways of living to those of a more sophisticated kind, from subsistence to cash economies, to the adoption of the methods of modern science and technology — all require sacrifices in terms of hard work and acceptance of the need for discipline and team effort. There is a pressing need for both adaptation and innovation — which are equally demanding. People, everywhere, are quick to learn that a poor economic background, a low social status, and other disadvantages can be overcome by talent in sport. All sportsmen can experience single-minded dedication, and the satisfactions arising from self-discipline, teamwork and fairplay. For women, in particular, sport is a valued means of securing emancipation in society. It thus has immense potential as a medium for inducing change. In the context of the Third World in particular, the slogan 'sport for sport's sake only' seems both immoral and degenerate.

We must also be careful not to over-intellectualise man's development. Sport reminds us of the need for a truly balanced sensory education involving touch, taste, sight and hearing. It reminds us also of the need for fun in our lives. In the Third World education is for a minority — school based education, that is — and so informal ways of reaching people are sought. Is sport a much under-rated means of reaching people? Could it take the place of the extended family? Can sport groups help in the preservation of valuable cultural traditions? Can the sports and physical education curriculum ensure the continued development of folk dances and indigenous games? Can sport stimulate literacy at the second stage when people want to practise their new skill with language? Is not sport the medium for optimum health education?

Development rests on the twin pillars of economic development and human resource development. Modern human beings at work require clerical and office management skills, receptivity to new ideas, the skills of facility maintenance and operation, and acceptance of a time-oriented pattern of life. Such skills can be practised in sports situations and, even if they are not practised successfully, such failure is not crippling — as it might be if the skills were being practised in other critical areas of life. The transfer of such skills must, of course, be deliberately 'taught' — they are not transferred to life in general by accident. Some writers have suggested that games should become part of a conscious and determined effort to accelerate social change. Desmond Morris has written imaginatively about the importance of games and sports — as well as music, singing and dancing — as complex and specialised forms of exploration and experiment. He sees the function of this exploratory behaviour as being to provide man with a subtle and complex awareness of the world around him and of his own capacities. What is developed in this generalised way can be 'applied anywhere at any time'. There is the development of inventiveness and the beginning of the 'creative animal'. Such qualities are of obvious importance in societies struggling to develop.

Play contributes to an individual's personal growth and development. Play in 'nature' is play with objects in which the straight line, the square, all regular shapes do not appear; but could it not be that play with regular-shaped implements and involving balance and force can help to lay the basic patterns of a technological society?

The Third World countries have always been weighed down by the problem of unemployment — especially among young people who form such a large proportion of their people. This problem is becoming worldwide with great rapidity. People are asking if unemployment is to be a feature of modern life. If it is, how can we overcome the problems at the human level — let alone the economic level? People will suffer if they have no job; in societies which describe their members by job-labels such as doctor, teacher, engineer, banker, plumber, and so on, the 'out of work' human being is without status. His ego is crucified. Can we envisage a future society in which people describe themselves, in their time, as athlete, swimmer or tennis player, as well as artist, musician or writer?

Third World countries have often inherited political frontiers which do not tally with their natural, ethnic boundaries. Most of them are trying to integrate a population speaking many languages and inheriting diverse cultures. Left entirely to free development, sports — competitive sports, especially — can excite dangerous, even if dormant, feelings and antagonisms between racial groups. In such situations sports must be carefully controlled if they are to be of positive value to society. Singapore was one country which found it necessary to regulate the 'racial' structure of teams at school level. The country was divided into regions, and teams representing those regions contained children of Indian, Chinese, Malay and European origin — all mixed. Left to the traditional 'separate schools' system, sports matches were found to be a means of stimulating aggression with frightening spin-off effects. Controlled inter-racial organisation of sport was used to *teach* the importance of racial understanding and collaboration.

An extension of this is the use of sport in many countries of Africa, Asia and Latin America, to develop an understanding of national identity, and to foster community pride and development. A Brazilian once said to me: 'You English are lucky — you have a long history. You have won great battles, you know what it is to feel English. We are a young country; we have many races and many languages and cultures. But when we win the World Cup we *know* what it is to feel Brazilian.'

I want to return now to two countries of Eastern Europe, considering especially their sports administration: Bulgaria and Poland.

The Bulgarian Union of Physical Culture and Sports is funded by three main agencies — the *toto* lottery (based on football or, failing that, on numbers), which has ploughed the equivalent of tens of millions of pounds into Bulgarian sport over the last twelve years; donations from the trade unions; and state subsidies. Since facilities are all community-owned, profits from ticket sales are also put back into the sport. The President of the Union is always an eminent person 'close' to the Prime Minister, and he has the status of a Minister. Other bodies which enjoy this relationship include those for tourism, for automobiles, and for culture. A major congress of the Union takes place every five years; there is an annual meeting of the 170-strong central council and every two months a meeting of a smaller elected committee from this council. A nine-member presidency meets every two weeks. The secretariat of the Union has the normal committees for bodies of this kind: for planning, for organisation, for facilities, etc., and a special committee for high-performance sport. Among representatives serving on the Union are those from the sports federations, the Rector of the High School for Physical Culture, the Deputy Minister of Education, the 320 multi-sport clubs in the country, sports medical and sports science delegates, and sports writers. Trade unions and the youth organisations, in addition to the Communist Party, all take a serious interest in sport. Bulgarian representation at intergovernmental sports meetings organised by Unesco are determined by the Bulgarian National Commission for Unesco on which sits a member for sport (the International Director of the Bulgarian Olympic Committee as it happens). The Bulgarian Olympic Committee is organised entirely separately. Among the difficulties identified by a spokesman for Bulgarian sport are: procedural rivalries between various groups within this overall structure, the need to give sports federations more autonomy, and the need for improved collaboration at local level in sports provision. Scientific journals and a national sports newspaper are published by the Union, and the curriculum of the High School for Physical Culture is directly related to Union decisions.

In Poland until about 1977 there was a Ministry of Sport and Tourism. A small percentage of the foreign tourist earnings of the country paid for all the overseas travel of Polish international teams. Then, except at local level in all but a few large tourist regions, this connection between sport and tourism was ended. The general opinion is that this was unfortunate for sport. Funding again is from state subsidies, the *toto* lottery, ticket sales and sports promotions, and profits from the many factories making sports goods. At local level there is substantial financial aid to clubs, and trade unions are again heavily involved in sport. The President of the supreme body for Polish sport — the General Committee for Physical Culture and Sport — is again of eminent rank and has the same status as other Presidents of national organisations, e.g. of the General Committee for Tourism. The General Committee has in its membership the Deputy Ministers of

Education, Health, Trade, Defence and the Interior. The seven High Schools of Physical Culture are represented, as are the Council of Science in Sport, the Sport for All Society (more than 1 million registered members), the Rural Sports Society (again more than 1 million members), and other organisations and persons likely to contribute to the overall efficiency of Polish sport. In theory the Olympic Committee is independent, but as in many countries the salaries of some officials are met from subsidies from the General Committee, and its President is often the President of the General Committee. The General Committee again has its planning, financial and other specialised sub-committees and employs about 200 persons directly in its Warsaw administration. Multi-sport clubs connected in a loose way with the Army, the Police, the trade unions and factories are the norm, but 'associate membership' for people outside these organisations, available through introduction by a member, means that most real enthusiasts are satisfied (the same thing happens increasingly with industrial sports clubs in Britain). The High Schools train teachers of physical education and coaches. A growth area is in health, fitness and rehabilitation studies in the High Schools, which qualify graduates for work in the sports centres, hospitals and trade union health centres. The General Committee also has its high-performance unit which, among other tasks, ensures adequate sports medical provision, and finances the several sports training centres in the country, by the sea and in the mountains. Sports newspapers are not published by the General Committee but by separate publishing companies; there is unfettered debate in their columns. The Committee does, however, fund scientific sports journals, and an excellent sports research institute attached to the Warsaw Academy of Physical Culture. In addition to the high-performance unit, there are other major units in the General Committee specialising in such areas as foreign affairs, schools sport, and sports equipment. There are no special arrangements with the Polish National Airline for ticketage, I am told on good authority, and there are no special reductions for sports groups on internal transport, although there are useful arrangements for youth groups and others; transportation within the country is relatively cheap anyway. In the fifty-nine districts of Poland there are Departments of Sport and Tourism, except for five centres where sport and tourism have been divided. The professional staff employed are paid by the Civic authorities and these have a token representation on the General Committee.

Among the problems encountered by modern Polish sports organisers are the following. First, there is a need to streamline the sports medical liaison between the Ministry of Health and the General Committee; there are conflicts between experts in the Ministry of Education, and between the educationists and others, who fear the adverse influence on children of 'prima donnas' in the sports clubs. There is also the feeling that there are 'too many organisers' of Polish sport; nevertheless it is realised that 'a little anarchy means, actually, more money'! The question of leading stars in some sports and their relationship to the international sports circuit has also to be resolved ideologically. For example Woytek Fibak, the tennis player, has no restrictions placed on his earnings. There is no law forbidding overseas earnings by Poles in this way; in this, sport is compared to art. The Polish national airline LOT also sponsors Fibak. Although not legally bound to contribute to Polish tennis, Fibak does organise exhibition matches against world players from time to time and donates equipment to his tennis federation. In some other East European countries there are, I believe, laws governing such relationships. International rules regarding double taxation also affect tennis players from Eastern Europe, as they do those from elsewhere. Fibak is accorded generous flexibility concerning his law studies at Cracow University. Lastly, the Poles have some interesting ways of funding their Olympic efforts. In addition to the funds arising from Polish Olympic Clubs abroad, a small percentage of the gate money from all sports matches in Poland goes to the National Olympic Committee, and there are two special contributions each year from the national *toto* lottery.

So much for these glimpses into a world reservoir of sporting ideas and actualities. I have given a few impressions, and for the serious student of sport I have merely thrown up a few signposts. There is a lifetime of research awaiting the enthusiast here. The pressing problem for Britain is how to design a strategy for its own sport; how to profit from this world reservoir of knowledge; and how to protect and enhance its own unique sports culture, which it shares with the Commonwealth. The outlining of a possible strategy for British sport thus makes up the final chapter of this essay.

11

A STRATEGY FOR BRITISH SPORT

'No matter if a tree grows to more than a thousand feet in height, each leaf, every day, must return to its roots for nourishment.'

— *Chinese Buddhist proverb*

Let us go back to our sporting roots. We have the longest history of organised competitive sport in the modern era. The reasons for this are many: that most modern competitive sports originated in the British Isles; that Britons were the foremost exporters of games and sports; and that British educationists were leading proponents of the idea that sport was part of a truly balanced education. Where-ever we look, if we look closely, we often find that what is now common in sport the world over had a root, if only a tenuous one, in these islands. It is an astonishing story, a part of our cultural heritage of which we should be proud — and which we should protect enthusiastically.

These sports began at different times and in different ways, and kept to themselves. This insularity finds eloquent expression in the museums of tennis at Wimbledon and of cricket at Lords: there is no British Museum of World Sport — we ought to have one as I have been urging for thirty years. Inter-sport insularity is also the reason why it is so difficult for British sport to react with one voice to the South African question.

The principle of 'do it yourself', of self-help, of participatory democracy is another British invention in sport. We have never needed a 'Father of Gymnastics' like the Germans (F.L. Jahn), or a 'Father of Games' like the Swedes (Viktor Balck). Our sports have been based on the notion that those who play them should also organise themselves — at club level, at school level and, until recently, at national and international level. During the war, in Watford where I lived, most male teachers were called up into the armed forces. We had to decide whether to organise the Under-16 soccer matches in the town or let them go; we decided that we, the boys, would organise them largely ourselves. And so we did.

This principle expressed itself most forcefully in the world of higher education; a pattern of sports self-government by the students which was a model for the world. The rowing training camps enjoyed by Oxford and Cambridge rowing teams — and rightly so — as preparation for the annual boat race are another 'invention' — not those of some machiavellian foreign power. Like the Greek athletes of antiquity, the oarsmen are *expected* to bring their art and skill to a high level of refinement before competition. Most academics in sport also received 'broken-time' payments. For example, a university teacher might have two months free in the summer, coinciding with the athletics seasons. Such a person could take part in a full programme of training and competition anywhere in the world without loss of pay. Not so the wage earner — the person who clocks on and off daily. His 'earning time' is broken. If he is recompensed he could suffer disqualification from amateur sport as a 'professional'. This is the nub of the question.

Much has been done to solve this problem, but as a general question it still lacks a proper solution. Many leading sportsmen have also found excellent jobs through sport; it was not unknown for an ambitious politician to exploit his athletics prowess to improve his chances of being selected as a parliamentary candidate; it is the case that one leading athlete was sent to the United States by the Foreign Office on a goodwill tour to bolster Britain's image. I am sure that more than one prominent sportsman has been taken aside by a political manager and told something like 'play your cards right and you can be assured a safe seat, and probably high office as well. The world is your oyster — but keep on winning!' In journalism, television and public relations, sports prowess has been the basis of many careers.

Again, special sports schools are not an East German or Soviet invention. The 'sports scholarship', in a soft-sell way, has long been known at our oldest universities, and ability at rugby has long been *one* of the criteria taken into consideration at medical schools. I know of one aspiring mathematics master whose selection from among a number of equal candidates eventually rested on his ability to hold his own at tennis with the headmaster!

Many public schools set out to make a name for themselves through sports success. Millfield, for example, is unashamedly a 'special sports school'. If a parent can afford the enormous fees, a child can enjoy the neo-Olympian education available there. Some, precocious and with mighty talent, can enjoy it through scholarships and subsidies. The merits of the multi-sport, multi-culture, all-family 'club' like Hurlingham have already been expounded, but even at local level in an urban area of deprivation we can count another 'first' — the Peckham Health Centre, which a group of researchers established just before the Second World War to help in the studies on 'social health'. In return for co-operation in the research projects, families in the area could enjoy the swimming, gymnastics, table tennis, darts, cards, crêches and other facilities provided free. This was a most advanced concept much enjoyed by the people of Peckham. Eventually the project died through lack of funding. There was also a lack of conviction among some of the sports and recreation leaders in the late 1940s and early 1950s; I was once told sharply by a recreation leader of national repute that he was 'against the underlying principle involved'. A great pity since 'Peckham Health Centres' are what all inner city neighbourhoods badly need. Centres where all people can enjoy exercise, skill training at all levels, and company, under qualified leadership; and at points every two miles down the Old Kent Road and other roads like it in all our cities.

Gordonstoun is another school which builds much of its reputation on excellence in outdoor sports and recreation. The 'Outward Bound' type of institution, is now common; almost every local authority and even some state comprehensive schools have their 'mountain centre', is an extension of the Gordonstoun philosophy. The Inner London Education Authority has its outdoor centre in North Wales; Crown Woods Comprehensive School in Eltham has its own outdoor 'lodge' in Scotland. Outdoor education has now become something in its own right rather than a mere adjunct of physical education. It would be a pity if economies were to hit hard at areas such as this, and were to hold back a momentum which has been increasing for more than twenty years throughout the country. Perhaps 'communion with nature' and 'survival education', two pillars of the outdoor education movement, are pointing the way forcefully for education in general. It is strange that we are so slow to recognise this.

We were early into sports administration at international level; two Britons were in the first International Olympic Committee. Football pools began here and were copied worldwide — to the benefit of the recipient-nations' sports organisations; only here have we allowed the Pools Promoters to dominate the scene.

We cannot say we were the first into the Colleges of Physical Education, but we can say that we housed the first which was exclusively for women — that established by the Swede Madame Osterberg. We can say that British women have utilised sports as a vehicle for wider political and social aims. Emancipation for women was won by many battalions — including violent commandos — but including also the non-militant 'gymnastic suffragettes'. In sports medicine we have a number of scalps. A.V. Hill wrote brilliantly early in the century on the science of athletics and the physiology of exercise, and his work remains valid.

The great Sherrington spurred disciples to apply his physiological theories to the nervous system of sportsmen in the search for new patterns of athletic skill. Our reputation in physical medicine is superb, but it has been the putting together of these ingredients into 'sports medicine' which has evaded us. Sports medicine still has no course for qualifying doctors who want to specialise in the area. However, the leading soccer clubs in Britain have long emphasised medical care of their players. The bigger clubs employ a full time physiotherapist — or two. Almost all have an honorary medical adviser and 'special arrangements' at the local hospital. Arsenal Football Club was one of the first clubs to utilise a mobile X-Ray unit so that injuries could be recognised immediately as serious or minor

Cross-country running was the mother of *fartlek*,* interval running and jogging. This remarkable sport for all has been the envy of many countries who point to our 'running culture' as the reservoir for British sports success.

In the establishment of coaching as a profession we made substantial progress early. Cricket and tennis coaches appeared in many private schools. The squash professional was also known. Golf professionals were everywhere. The mushrooming of swimming pools for the community was accompanied by 'instructors' at the pool-side; not *very* well qualified, and unstructured as a group, but there nevertheless.

We created the connection between industry and sport, especially in soccer; for example, Arsenal Football Club began life as Woolwich Arsenal at Plumstead — they were a 'works team' connected with the munitions factory there. We fostered the development of great soccer clubs from small church sports groups. Social leaders of their time, like the Royal Family and the Marquis of Exeter (formerly Lord Burghley) today and the Marquis of Queensberry in late Victorian times have patronised sport. We have surrounded selected sports events with all the trappings of a magnificent ceremonial — Henley, Wimbledon, the Open, the Cup Final.

It was all there; almost everything which we now see blooming elsewhere *started* here. But unfortunately, it stopped short; it was never fully democratised, being restricted to a few privileged

*A Swedish word meaning 'speed play'. It was 'invented' by the Swedish trainers concerned with the middle-distance runners Arne Anderson and Gunder Haegg — whose best performances were in the 1940s. When Geoffrey Dyson, national athletics coach in Britain in the late 1940s and early 1950s, visited Sweden to research this training method (it involves varying paced training over country), the Swedes explained that their 'invention' was a variation of the method used by the old English runner W.G. George who was active early this century!

groups. Conceptions like 'amateurism' were negative inventions intended to exclude certain social groups. One can still see the process at work. The 'quality' press still reports polo and rackets — almost regularly; rarely does it report fully those rapidly developing members of the world and mass-sport fraternity such as volleyball, handball and basketball. The ceremonial events also have an irritating twist in the tail. As historical survivals I applaud them, but as evidence of sporting excellence I find them abhorrent. The Oxford and Cambridge crews should not maquerade as rowing *champions*, and the media should ensure that the difference is well understood. There must be many other university crews who would be in the running were this a university rowing championship.

Although we were the first to see how sport can profit from the enormous brainpower brought in by the volunteer organiser, we must make sure that future British sport is not just the last refuge of the 'establishment'. The patrons of British sport are still largely aristocratic at the figurehead level; this is a fact, and many people seem to prefer it this way. This is not 'non-political'; monarchism, from which it stems, is a political creed. Perhaps there should be more balancing with people eminent in totally different spheres. *Our first task in creating a strategy for British sport then, is to track our sporting heritage back to its roots and then fully democratise it.*

At this point, lest my criticism be thought merely carping, let me pay tribute to something else in British sports culture; the freedom to do one's own thing. It is a valuable freedom and one which has enabled me to travel the world to research and write, and to compete; and, of course, to write this book. I value this freedom, exploit it to the hilt, and want to perpetuate it. Nevertheless, I hope that if my individual idiosyncrasies are likely to cause grave hurt to Britain's overall sporting image or its standing generally in the world, someone will restrict my actions!

As part of the process of identifying these sporting roots I was asked to give my views in a recent comparative exercise (UK/USSR Educational Exchanges Joint Communiqué, 26 January 1977, London). I first listed those areas in which I thought we had something of substantial interest to learn from the Soviet Union. These included several Olympic sports like gymnastics and basketball; centres of excellence and early selection procedures; sports health resorts; and sports in factories and offices and for the elderly. I thought we had something to learn about research, particularly in the area of 'autogenic' and other psychological training methods. Similarly in massage, rehabilitation, climatology and balneology (forms of bathing). There was the matter of trade union involvement in sport; I have always thought that a trade union could do much more for its members by raising the day-to-day—and leisure—'quality of life' than merely increasing the size of the pay packet.

I thought we might learn by a study of Soviet stadium use and ownership, about the organisation of large-scale sports festivals, and about links between sport and the arts. I also listed areas where the Soviet Union might learn something from us. There was the matter of the English language, used in all countries as the prime linguistic means of exchange: 'foul', 'offside' and 'goal' come loud and clear from terraces in Kiev and Leningrad, as well as in Britain (we could give more thought to simplifying the use of the English language in the world of international sport). We had so much of value in terms of sports history and student sports organisation. Our own developments in sport for the handicapped, especially paraplegics, was world-famous. In some sports like hockey and rugby we still had things to teach them. We had some interesting ideas on the environment and the role of sport in outdoor education and conservation. We provided a positive environment for the growth of many 'fringe' activities related to sports and exercise: the Alexander* techniques of postural re-education, Feldenkrais** gymnastics, meditation, diet, naturopathy, vegetarianism, relaxation techniques, 'inner sport'† and other 'way out' disciplines. We still had our public parks to show, with their generous provision of play areas and tennis courts. We had the unique Public Footpaths Protection Acts on our statute books, evidenced in our leisure practice. There was the tradition of allowing small groups of sports lovers to develop their own clubs; the system of supplementing these initiatives with local and national state subsidies. There was so much of which we could be proud.

Thirdly, there were areas where both countries could have profitable exchanges of opinion: the question of sport and physical education in the schools and the training of specialist teachers, coaches and administrators; the provision of structured training for children and adults at the 'middle level' of skill and ability; arguments concerning what is élitism and what is the search for excellence. There was the important matter of defining and analysing the conflict-points in world sports politics—and trying to advance towards lasting solutions. Too many of these problems are handled

*A pioneer in postural education. His work is being continued in London by Dr. Wilfred Barlow, whose book *The Alexander Principle* was published by Gollancz in 1973.

**A teacher of movement, especially for the handicapped. See his *Awareness through movement* (Harper and Row, New York, 1972).

†See G. Leonard, *The Ultimate Athlete* (Viking Press, New York, 1974).

'off the cuff' by badly briefed, honorary committees, working on the thinking-aloud and show-of-hands principle. Incredible!

A similar exercise could be conducted with the United States, with the Scandinavian countries and throughout the Commonwealth. So the second task I see for those elaborating a strategy for British sport is *the identification of those aspects of the world sporting pattern into which we most wish to absorb ourselves*.

We have to do this objectively, bearing in mind — arising from our first task — that there will be traditional elements in our own national sporting pattern which we wish to protect. I imagine cricket will be with us for a few more years! And there are other sports which bind us closely to the Commonwealth in sport.

But we have to take firm decisions about our international involvement. Do we wish to emphasise a balanced approach to the full twenty-six sports on the Olympic programme? Or are we going to be selective? What will be our criteria for selection? We might choose our past history — our strengths in soccer, in middle-distance running, in rowing and sailing. There *is* something to be said for an island emphasising water sports at both mass and championship levels; and there is something to be said for a narrow approach so that we have some goods which still draw gasps of admiration in the shop window of world competitive sport.

Our third task is to think out our sport ideology. What do we require from sport in a complex and modern society? Is 'sport for sport's sake' still valid, or is it mere rhetoric? Do we accept that modern sports relationships provide a unique means for persons and states to interact symbolically? Do we agree that sport balances education by reminding the intellectuals that the senses have an equal need; that sport advances the struggle for personal and community health, being clearly on the side of those who *counter* groups which promote anti-health products as socially normal and approved? Do we agree that those who finally dot the *i*'s and cross the *t*'s of this ideology should be fully aware that sport belongs to everyone? — and that the forces of private freedom and initiative should be balanced by those of national interest and community development? A British ideology for sport must reflect all these tendencies — it will be a final package made up of a sophisticated mixture of approximations and balances.

Our ideology will recognise the unity of sport — a whole more important than the sum of separate-sport parts. It will be concerned with international thinking and solidarity in sport. It will protect and enhance the high regard which other countries still have for the British in the field of sport and sports organisation. It will challenge sportsmen to recognise a healthy patriotism — the pride of representing one's community, and one's culture, in an international forum. I once asked Jaroslav Drobny the Czech Wimbledon singles champion and long a British resident, why, since he had been invited to coach the Egyptian and Iranian national teams, he had never been asked to help with the British. He said 'I would never have anyone in my team who wanted money to represent his country. I would start with the youngsters again and teach them proper behaviour.' Enough said.

Our ideology will recognise sport's place in society, its contribution to personal and community health. It will recognise that for some people sport is a form of 'work', but we will contrive ways that enable people both to maintain their own professions and to practise sport at a high level. Most top sportsmen are happier when they have a job to fall back on. Not only does this make them happier by helping them to avoid the mad rush to affluence before the ageing process overtakes them, but I am sure it makes them better sportsmen. Most athletes are hypochondriacs; if they have nothing else but sport to think about they become super-hypochondriacs! Similarly with sports administration; it is important to have those with management and public relations flair in sports management. It is as important to maintain the tradition of the part-timer, voluntary and elected, among sports officials as among the sportsmen themselves. Sports-for-all is desirable; so is sports administration-for-all. Our present system of using the enthusiasts in sports administration brings a volume of brainpower to sport which it could not buy on the open employment market. It brings to sports organisation senior people from many professions. It helps us to utilise the retired — when retirement seems to be getting ever earlier. These people are glad to be of service to a cause they love; nevertheless, some financial and secretarial help should be provided to help them in their public service.

Our ideology will recognise also the involvement of industry and commerce in sport. Commercial thinking can be imaginative and lively; sport needs it, but it cannot rely entirely on the whims and fancies of the market-place. It must have a permanence and continuity which only institutional backing can provide. The driving wheel of the sports movement must rest firmly in the hands of those who teach sport and those who are elected and appointed to direct it.

We cannot wait until this ideology is fully worked out before taking *action*. There are areas where action is urgently needed, and can be taken immediately. The major sticking point is the *national administration of sport*. A decision to end the petty squabbling and power struggles can and should be made, but it will not be effective until the various personalities and groups concerned share objectives and targets. I come back again to the Olympic Games of 1988. There could be no better target than that, and let us hope that at the 1981 Baden-Baden Olympic Congress — where a decision on the 1988 Games will be made — a British bid is made and accepted. We would then have the possibility of a seven-year programme of action leading up to an event of world importance; such a programme might also be graced with a Commonwealth Games based in the United Kingdom in 1986. The cutting edge of the administrative machine would no longer be at issue; it would be the British Olympic Association nominated as the host organiser by the International Olympic Committee. The British Olympic Association would have to boost its forces. The London Olympics Organising Committee would be stronger and more widely based than the current BOA; it would include representatives of the state and of London government; it would include those responsible for security, accommodation, publicity, finance, transportation and related activities. But the cutting edge would have been identified. There are of course many other valid arguments as to why this should be so; to recapitulate — the British Olympic Association is the oldest of the British multi-sport bodies; it is the only truly *British* organisation; its membership is open to institutions *and* individuals; it is open to Olympic sports and non-Olympic sports; it is concerned with élite sport and mass sport; it has health and education as concurrent objectives; it has a special role in cultivating the fine arts.

Behind the cutting edge should be rallied the Sports Council; the Sports Councils for Scotland, Wales and the regions; and the Central Council for Physical Recreation. There must, surely, be work for them all? In the working together for a common aim, patterns of co-operation will be laid and practised, and a common working practice will itself lead to a long-term solution to the problem of administering British sport. To my mind this would be the ideal solution.

But what if we do not bid for, or for some other reason do not get the 1988 Olympic Games? Will the Central Council of Physical Recreation lie down and be quiet? I doubt it. Many feel that the sports federations and other interested bodies do have a rightful place; that the elective structure of a CCPR-type body must be recognised, and rewarded with power. Will the Sports Council modify its 'octopus complex' and stop trying to gobble up almost all areas of sporting enterprise? And will it remember that it administers public money — not its own? Will it be able so to modify its behaviour that it can win the confidence of the whole sporting movement? Would acting as a kindly uncle be one way? Or taking a stance analogous to the Arts Council which does not seem to crave publicity or recognition in a neurotic way? Would a reversion to the original conception — a small body advising the Minister on sports policy in general and being the watchdog for public accountability over financial grants to sport — be the answer? It is unrealistic for the CCPR to boast that it is the perfect democratic model of sports administration, and it is pointless for the Sports Council to continue acting as if it were an *elected* body — *chosen* to be the leader of British sport. In our society I see no acceptable alternative to an *elected* sports administrative body — even one with a 51:49 ratio in favour of elected representatives.

Again the British Olympic Association might be utilised as the marriage broker. The United States Congressional Committee which recently considered sports administration called for one national sports body. It concluded that the United States Olympic Committee was to be that body; the USOC was asked to bring together the warring Amateur Athletic Union and National Collegiate Athletics Association. Could it be that the non-threatening British Olympic Association — a highly democratic elected body with power in the hands of the representatives of the twenty-six Olympic sports — could provide a British answer, whether or not we get the 1988 Olympic Games? Certainly the BOA cannot be left out. After all, it mounts a campaign every four years to promote British participation in the Olympic Games. Its ongoing educational programme is also increasing. Its continuing role and its independence are protected by its constitutional links with the International Olympic movement.

We have a fourth factor — the Minister of Sport and Recreation. Government control is a sensitive matter in British sport. Perhaps we in sport are too sensitive. Instead of for ever prattling about the danger of connections between sport and government, we might protect our freedoms more by accepting that those connections *do* exist — and must be faced squarely. Can the Minister of Sport be the broker? However, to choose one body, unilaterally, without discussion is no long-term answer.

There are too few opportunities for discussion in British sport, a situation by which I have long been worried and irritated. When our representatives speak for Britain in the Unesco Inter-Governmental Committee on Sport, *how* do they speak? How do they cast their votes? How have they been briefed? What action have they taken to ascertain opinion in the country, in the federations, in the clubs, in the colleges of physical education? What attempts are made to evaluate such missions and to make the results of the debates more widely known? To whom are our delegates accountable? Who *are* our delegates anyway? Owing to the diversity of organisations there is no easy way of finding out who represents us — what they say and what reports they make when they return. The same questions arise over delegates to other international conferences on sport and physical education. This is an area of casualness and weakness. We have the right to know how our delegates vote and think in the councils of international sporting life.

At this stage let me say that I do not have an *absolute* belief in government by election and committee. We are all aware in sport no less than in other spheres — how persons are elected to positions of power and then become almost invulnerable and established for life. The officers of an organisation might be stifled by power-hungry 'amateur officials'; they might, themselves, launch out on uncontrolled, malicious and vengeful paths. Into any structure must, I suggest, be injected *individuals* who are respected for their knowledge, ability and utter credibility. Luckily we still have a number of these in the British sports family. The British Olympic Association has strengthened its authority and image by becoming fully representative — at National Olympic Committee level — of the twenty-six Olympic sports. This is a big advance on the previous NOC, which was too much an 'old boy' network. Nevertheless it could still be improved, I venture to suggest, by a clause which allowed for a small number of individuals to serve as full members.

This solution to the problem of British sports administration is a convergent one. Are there alternatives of a more innovative and divergent kind? Might we not de-centralise the whole sports administrative network? A parliament of national sports could then be built up by representatives from more than 400 sports centres. Should we not grasp the amateur-professional nettle firmly and *transform* the professional soccer club? By astute tax changes, management innovations and conceptual changes, the soccer club could itself become a community sports centre of great worth — and with a future brighter than that which is promised for most of them at the moment. A federated structure of local 'clubs' of this kind is not unrealistic.

We might think about decentralising still further. The schools and universities are still our main source for sports development — a fact which professional sports must be made to recognise. The Sports Council might consider a powerful drive in this area; the aim being to create in factories facilities, staffing and organisation similar to that found in universities and colleges. I have spelt this out earlier in this book. In short, for the sports lover going to work would be like going to university. In working time, on the spot, with coaching, and in clean and attractive surroundings, there would be the possibility of daily involvement in sport and exercise. The argument that people prefer to take their sport outside places of work is a red herring: of course they do — but as well as, not instead of, excellent sports provision *at* work. Just recently I have been occupied in considering how British schools might be involved in the 1980 Olympic appeal. I am coming round to the conclusion that every school should have an 'Olympic attaché' to co-ordinate activities, raise funds, and develop the Olympic idea in all its forms. Why could this not be a permanent feature of all educational establishments and larger places of work? Such a network would be invaluable to sports administrators for spreading their message, and for receiving feedback; and not only in Olympic years. New ways of bringing young people into sports planning and policy decisions must be found. A National Youth Council for Sport could be one of several special-interest sports 'think tanks'.

Administration is, of course, only part of the answer to leadership in sport. We have struggled on with a faulty administrative system for so long that it would be almost disturbing to live with anything better. However, there are now other categories of leadership which could be called 'sports management'. These include the managers of recreation and sports centres, and professional administrators of national sports organisations. The former are now organised professionally; there are several organisations, and the Association of Recreation Managers is a major one. Their hands are tied while the philosophy of profit is the dominant one pervading local sport, i.e. that a sports centre is concerned more with throughput and fees, and less with social service and health. However the basis of a national network, which could be inspiring for sport in the front line, does exist.

Leadership is also intimately concerned with motivation and thus with the media. It has long surprised me that the sports press is not more involved with sports planning and strategy. Apart from professional physical education groups in colleges and universities, the sports press are perhaps the only people professionally involved in 'thinking about sport'. It is easy for this intelligent group to sit on the sidelines and use their intelligence destructively. It would be to the mutual benefit of sport and the sports media if better ways could be found of bringing the journalists and the commentators into the planning process.

The media also have enormous responsibility. They cannot be proud of themselves and their history in sports leadership. Sport is seen as fair game for comment — mostly destructive comment if this improves the reading or viewing figures. The media have a leadership role; they should try to set leads as well as follow them. A major and immediate contribution of the sports media collectively would be the production of a national sports newspaper — perhaps subsidised by the Sports Council. Certainly this is badly needed; it would help remove the country's insularity in world sport and the insularity of each sport *vis-à-vis* the others. I pray for the day when a national newspaper in Britain will present, regularly, a truly balanced coverage of sport, and when the so-called 'minor sports' have their national league results exposed *regularly* to the viewing public.

For a truly world view of sport one turns to the French *L'Equipe* or other continental newspapers. The US *Sports Illustrated* is another 'opinion-forming' sports spectacular, with strong North American bias but with international coverage. The British sports press generally, as you can see almost any day in the popular press, is unbalanced in its sports content. I do not object to the space given to soccer since this *is* the national game. Racing news takes up more than most human sports and in some newspapers greyhound news has strong support, reflecting the British tendency to provide more sporting facilities for horses and dogs than for human beings. In athletics our best runners are encouraged to take a prima donna attitude; personality cults are eagerly fostered. This kind of build-up often effectively spoils the chances of our athletes in Olympic and international competition; they cannot live up to expectations created by some sections of the media. Of course Sebastian Coe and Steve Ovett are wonderful athletes; but so will be all other finalists in world events. Any one of them can win on the day; but any one of them can have an off-day or a pulled muscle. We hear so little in the British sports press of their international rivals that a foreign winner comes over almost as a beginner who had no right to his victory. In September 1979 the World Student Games were held in Mexico City; there were only fleeting reports in the British sports press although we had a team representing us. In the *majority* of world sports international coverage is only cursory. The Mediterranean Games held in Yugoslavia in September 1979 involved fourteen countries: one would have thought them worth at least a mention.

The situation is better than it was and I feel it will get better. Many sports journalists want the situation to improve. It boils down always to the question of aim: should the sports media only *follow* public opinion — or should it *lead*? It must do both — but at present the balance is tilted towards *following*. I greatly admire the intellectual calibre of our best sports writers; I want to profit more from their knowledge and advice and I want to create an administrative structure which makes this possible — without muting their necessary criticism. Over the years since I started writing (as 'Anthony MacDonald', Sports Editor, *Cyprus Sunday Times*, Nicosia, 1949/50) I have learnt much from journalists, and have come to admire their professionalism and discipline.

At this stage I must reinforce my plea for coaching as a profession. 'For every facility — a teacher' must be our clarion call. Every facility needs a *person* to breathe life into it. We need coaching in every public park which has tennis courts — not only for young people with time on their hands, but for adults wishing to learn a new skill. Both private (industrial) and state facilities should look for improvements here. Although there has been a little progress, we have much to do; we also have to study the employee-employer relationships in coaching. A coach cannot work his best as a local government employee as presently understood. The relationship of a *teacher* to a local authority is better. A coach needs the freedom to experiment; the very opposite of a 9-to-5 mentality and the conditions of employment that go with it. He needs the dignity of a creative worker. To try to establish a profession nationally in any less promising environment would be pointless.

Leadership also needs the participation of *everyone*. We need to improve our 'opinion gathering' on a national scale. Sport belongs to everyone and so we want everyone to think about sport — its meanings and purposes in society. 'Think tanks' should be common and their results communicated — and considered — in a co-ordinated and serious manner.

Lastly I return to teaching sport and physical education in education. If this is inspirational, dedicated, scientific, and not spoilt by over-complicating intellectualism, our national sports movement will continue to have living roots. Since 'sport' has become one of more than a dozen subjects in the school curriculum — and less a part of the mind-body-soul trinity — the unique role of the physical education specialist has suffered. We need, urgently, to recapture this uniqueness. A recent report by Department of Education and Science Inspectors (*Curriculum 11-16* [Supplementary Working Papers], June 1979) underlines this. It identifies seven skills which contribute to 'psycho-motor' competence: skills of posture; fine manipulative skills; skills of dealing with large objects and projectiles; gross motor skills including balancing, jumping, turning, climbing, swimming and running; techniques for dealing with a challenging environment — e.g. rock climbing and canoeing; artistic skills as expressed in various dance forms; and communication skills involved in non-verbal communication, such as gesture.

Theoretically, students and teachers are trained in these areas. In practice the very time allotment for physical education prevents theory becoming actuality. The time allotment in most schools is pitiful. A growing child would need a minimum of two hours per day of physical activity. This is a guess because no-one, to my knowledge, has fully researched the problem with finality. It is not the purpose of this book to spell out in detail the content of such a programme; I merely want to outline the major principles involved. The first two are: committed teachers of physical education who inculcate the desire for a lifelong participation in exercise, body care and sport; and an educational curriculum which allows for daily practice long enough to do some good. For the wrong reasons — the energy crisis and the resulting difficulty in keeping schools warm, and a shortage of teachers in schools — there are now suggestions for a major reform of the timetable. These wrong reasons could, however, result in an excellent framework for the teaching of sport and physical education. With mornings devoted to academic work, interspersed with short breaks, and afternoons given over entirely to sport and hobbies, the life of children in the United Kingdom would be revolutionised. It would herald a welcome return to the body — a body-centred education which was once the envy of the world and could be again. Teachers of physical education would work mainly in afternoons and evenings, especially as 'lifelong education' becomes normal, and responsibility moves towards the community equally with the school. The work of teachers and sports coaches would also become better co-ordinated, and the concept of 'centres of excellence' would be a possibility for every *locality* — rather than *region*. Should educational planning move in the future towards the true shared use of facilities, with one schools group using the buildings in the mornings and another in the afternoon (an idea also mooted), all is not lost. A three-part organisation of the day also has much to commend it. Teachers and children would work for two of those parts. Such planning would enable us to allow for the findings of modern biorhythmic research; children and teachers would work at their highpoints — emotionally, intellectually and physically. Unfortunately, at the time of writing it is likely that economies by local authorities will hit sports hard. A report in the *Observer* during September 1979 shows that 75 per cent of volleyball clubs in Scotland face the prospect of being made homeless if gymnasia owned by schools and colleges are closed early to 'save energy'. Colleges in London have been asked to consider not timetabling the gymnasia/sports halls on two afternoons a week; similar developments are reported from Sheffield and Bristol. A Nottingham First League volleyball club is reduced to one hour's training a week. (At the same time the cost of hiring sports halls is mounting alarmingly.) Basketball, volleyball and badminton are sports affected by this policy.

A professor of music asked me recently: 'Why have you retreated from the College of Physical Education idea?' In music, he explained, the very best musicians go to a College of Music to develop their abilities. Should they wish to take up a teaching or academic career later, they can move sideways. Other people interested in music go for a degree in music. Such has been the passion for academic respectability that our traditional Colleges of Physical Education have been closed, changed or emasculated. Every new student is now registered for a degree, like it or not. In physical education we have to ask ourselves such questions as — Are we too concerned with 'A' level performance and not enough with motor performance? Can physical education be studied exactly as other academic subjects with 50 per cent of time designated 'non-contact' (i.e. no contact between the teacher and the taught — a principle in fashion in many colleges today)? Is it possible to compare the many different qualifications in physical education/movement studies and give guidance to potential employers?

Professional associations for teachers of physical education compete with each other for publicity and membership. Here too collaboration and co-ordination are needed. An equivalent of the British Medical Association is called for: one professional body to validate qualifications, offer opportunities for further studies, provide an authoritative journal and yearbook, engage in international placings for students and teachers, and conduct the host of matters which are necessary for a thriving professional body. We need a national policy for schools physical education which takes into account the development of a *continuous* national policy for sport. Assuming that we can agree on a core element in our national sports life in which everyone shares and which relates to world trends and needs, yet which reflects our whole culture, in its national and commonwealth setting, and does not banish individual idiosyncrasy, is it too much to ask that the physical education profession should nourish this core? The schools curriculum should relate closely to the community sports policy, for the mutual benefit of both.

To recapitulate on *facilities*. Ideally we are looking for exercise facilities and sports possibilities in the home and in the workplace, locally, regionally and nationally. Much here would have to be left to private enterprise, but if a facility were provided for the home by design, there is more likelihood that we would use it — just as 'granny flats' could see the end of old people's homes.

Facilities provide opportunities for all those who want merely to be left alone to organise their own activity, those who require elementary teaching, those in need of structured coaching, and the high flyer for whom the sky is the limit. I include in this thinking of course also those who need adapted physical education, postural re-education, slimming guidance, and so on. To meet these needs we must ensure that the present public and private facilities are made available. Such expressions of opinion have been made by successive governments over the last thirty years, to no avail. We *must* overcome this problem urgently.

We need more lateral thinking too. The idea of the pub becoming a sports centre has been gaining credence in the last ten years; a number of Sunday soccer teams now centre on a local pub. Much more could be done here by the brewing industry — especially as the warfare which the tobacco industry is experiencing is moving to the alcohol front! In Germany it is already recognised by insurance companies that 'fit' drivers are less prone to accidents. Some German motorway cafés, in addition to petrol pumps and shops, now have jogging trails — where tired and irritable drivers can take a quiet run. The huge shopping centres also present imaginative possibilities: during the Montreal Games a leading Canadian orchestra played to shoppers in a city shopping centre. It is my dream to take international sport to the ordinary people by holding a major volleyball event in a major shopping complex. I know of a major New York bank where an organist entertains the customers in the banking hall during the lunch period. How many other imaginative possibilities does this open up!

The transformation of the professional sports clubs will not come about by wishful thinking. The best and quickest transformation would result from an agreement by the Directors of professional soccer clubs that this should be so. What have they to lose — except, of course, their unchallenged power? They have much to gain. Their clubs would be important social centres; they would receive generous tax allowances; rates would be treated similarly. The more socially conscious they became, the better the allowances. Soccer would 'mother' other sports to mutual advantage. The 'match' would become the 'day': there would be gymnastics competitions in the mornings, basketball mid-day, followed by the normal soccer game. For the player there would be new horizons; for the vast majority of players the future is not attended by abundant wealth; in many ways it is sad and depressing, especially out of the big league. The true municipalisation of a soccer club could mean improved ways of integrating soccer players back into normal working life — better ways of protecting their health and their whole social future.

At the leisure end of sports facilities we should look for improvements. Some years ago a government report on (gardening) allotments called for a new look *vis-à-vis* play and recreation. The allotment holders would have access, collectively, to a small playground, a picnic area and other simple recreational facilities (for example, climbing frames and an outdoor 'circuit). Gardening would still be the main pursuit but the possibility of more permanent buildings and these recreational facilities would enable the whole family, occasionally, to join dad — or mum if it is she who is doing the digging!

The mushrooming of health clubs of various kinds has shown a great depth of interest. In addition to private action, we need increased corporate initiatives. I have in mind a network of centres comparable to the 'Bay Beach Club' in California where sport and exercise can be enjoyed in surroundings of splendour. It is unnecessary that the image of sport should be always mud, sweat and pain.

Looking outside the confines of pure sport, the tourist industry should take a close look at its future. There will be a big demand for the rejuvenated spa — the resort where one goes to devote two weeks to one's body, just as one gives a general 'service' to one's motorcar. At local level in industrial societies the trade unions and factory sports clubs should consider how they might involve their members and the local population surrounding their recreational facilities, in a continuous programme of activity. In this context such centres could be well used in providing 'supplement your child's physical education programme' sessions daily in the late afternoons, together with 'mother and child' family fitness groups in the mornings.

As for *programmes*, we do have some guidance. We are, officially, signatories to the Council of Europe 'European Sport for All Charter'. The principles of this Charter make interesting reading. Every individual shall have the right to participate in sport; public funding will underline the role sport plays in human development; sports planning shall be integrated with that in education, health, social services, the arts, leisure, conservation and other socio-cultural areas; there shall be permanent and effective co-operation between public and voluntary organisations in sport; sport shall be safeguarded and sportsmen protected from political, commercial and financial exploitation — and from practices that are 'abusive and degrading', including the unfair use of drugs (does this presuppose that there is a fair use of drugs?). The Charter continues:

there must be full use of existing and new facilities, and respect for local and regional differences in sports taste; access to open country and water for recreational purposes shall be protected, by legislation if necessary; in all programmes of sports development the need for fully qualified personnel at all levels of administration, management and coaching is recognised.

Not a bad programme; there is little in it to quarrel with. I would now like to see us set *targets* within this programme. It is the absence of targets which makes judgement so difficult. No targets — no possibility of measuring success or failure. A programme also needs colour, and this is best provided by national *campaigns* of some kind. The most recent campaigns for fitness were dampened by quarrels between the Health Education Council and the Sports Council, and the seeming inability of the Scottish and Welsh Councils to work with the (English) Sports Council. Campaigns should be regular features of the national sports programme, giving timely boosts to ongoing activities. Since 1979 a new factor has appeared on the British sports calendar — the British Olympic Day. This will be held every May Bank Holiday. The date was a good choice; it was a newly instituted Bank Holiday, and there was no traditional sports programme held on that day. Olympic sports would 'designate' an event in honour of the day — held actually on it or as near to it as possible. The spirit of the Jubilee multisport events in 1977 was pegged on to the British Olympic Day. Television took a real interest; the 1979 event was profitable in financial terms, although this was not the main intention. Here again we have a new and exciting project around which *all* sports administrative bodies could, and should, collaborate.

One cannot but return time and again to the problem of collaboration. We have no National Institute of Sport — an Institute to help administrative bodies devise the best programmes, facilities, leadership training, campaigns and other sports planning needs; and to be a source of information of all kinds in sport, from all countries. A National Sports Institute was conceived — for Loughborough University — but plans were thwarted, mainly by institutional rivalries. Sports medicine is also torn by disputes with at least three 'groups' not working harmoniously. These are the British Association of Sport and Medicine, the Institute of Sports Medicine, and the International Federation of Sports Medicine.

No one suggests that all action should be centralised into one institution. The history of our sports and sports administration makes this impossible — even if it were desirable. Work would go on wherever there are people and institutions capable of generating worthy ideas. But, every national programme needs a *cutting edge*—one cutting edge goes deeper than two or three. West Germany has Cologne, East Germany has Leipzig, and France has its Institut National des Sports. The United States is developing its Olympic Centre at Colorado Springs. Can *we* not have our cutting edge? And should it not be Loughborough? I make my judgement on the following grounds: Loughborough is the only British University with a Chair in Sports Sciences and Physical Education, hence it is the only one able to offer training and qualifications at *all* levels; it has a unique international reputation; it has an equally proud national reputation in sports; geographically it is almost exactly in the centre of England. If any other institution can offer a better combination of factors, I will reconsider this judgement! This does not, of course, exempt Loughborough from the need to change. It has, perhaps, gone overboard in the search for academic credibility; all our sports study institutions need to get back to grips with sports skills. I make a plea therefore that Loughborough should be the cutting edge for sports study, for sports medicine, and perhaps also for sports research and documentation—the three critical areas needing rapid and powerful development. This might be structured as an 'Institute' that is *at* but not *of* Loughborough University. The governing body of this Institute would be composed of representatives partly from other academic institutions with prc grammes of related activity; a model could be the Institute of Development Studies at Sussex University, which is funded mainly by the Ministry of Overseas Development but also by its own consultancy operations. Its governing body is composed of nationally noted experts. The fact that it is the cutting edge of development studies in this country does not inhibit the Universities of Wales at Swansea, East Anglia, Bradford and London, among others, from running courses in development studies. Much of the content of the Institute of Development Studies' journal is sometimes given over to explaining the work of the other institutes engaged in the same field of study. The 'cutting edge' structure has enabled the IDS to attain a world stature which it could never have attained had it been thwarted by national jealousies. Each of the sports 'Institutes' might be the hub of a national network; sports sciences; sports media; sports for the handicapped; and so on. Institutions, sports federations and individuals with expertise in their own right would feel that there was one focal point—one point into which they could feed their knowledge—and from which they might derive information and guidance. This structure has much to commend it—provided *it* did not develop an octopus complex and try to devour all other forms of enterprise. Another key to success will be the application of a true 'open doors' policy. The ideas of the best people available will be utilised; the Institutes will be accessible to all people who have something to say. The methods they use to screen submissions and debate opinions will be those best suited for mass communication. The major conference at which only *some*—those with a flair for public speaking but perhaps not the best brains—speak should not be the only means used to conduct work in matters of the mind.

It is such a cutting edge that the British *international* sports effort needs. It has long needed it. In 1959 I became involved in Unesco discussions on sport while covering the 'Unesco Conference on Sport, Work, and Culture' in Helsinki, for the (then) *Manchester Guardian* and *Sports Illustrated* (USA). In 1960 I wrote to the Unesco National Commission (now housed in the Ministry of Overseas Development) proposing a sport and physical education panel to advise our National Commission. I received a vague explanation which, in short, said that matters were in hand, there was no problem, and so on. I was to receive such a brush-off on many more occasions. In 1963 I elaborated a plan for improved international action for consideration by the General Secretary of the Central Council of Physical Recreation; again I was told that there was nothing for me to worry about!

With the establishment of the Sports Council I tried again; I sent a detailed memorandum proposing the establishment of a United Kingdom National Co-ordinating Centre for international physical education and sport. If the result was not complete silence, it was no more than quiet muttering. In 1972 the Government's Select Committee on Overseas Development published as an Appendix my memorandum on sports aid to developing countries. For the next three years I followed this up with letters to the Foreign and Commonwealth Office, the British Council and the Inner London Education Authority, among others. In 1976 a group of colleagues and I decided that the Central Bureau of Educational Visits and Exchanges would provide a fertile home for a 'Centre for International Sports Studies'. The Sports Council was consistently encouraged to join with us in this collective enterprise, now supported by almost all colleges and universities with projects in the area of international sports studies. Although individual members of the Sports Council have supported our efforts, any fully supportive institutional link has not been forthcoming.

We have organised two highly successful courses under the auspices of 'Olympic Solidarity', the first in 1976, held wholly at the Institute of Development Studies, University of Sussex, and the second in 1978 held in three centres: London, Loughborough

University, and the University of Sussex. We have links with more than seventy countries, including bilateral arrangements with Sudan, Jamaica, Libya and Indonesia. For the last-named we despatched, at very short notice, an expert on sports commentating to 'train' the local commentators for the South East Asian Games. We organised the first world seminar, in England, for directors of National Sports Stadia. We are drawing up plans for a Commonwealth Sports Trust or Foundation which will link voluntary to state action at grass roots level in sports and physical education development in the Commonwealth. We devised the idea of both services and studies; the services would eventually finance the studies. We are considering ways and means of working with commercial companies; the idea of 'sport for export', a means of linking sport with a British overseas export drive, has been supported. This is a far cry from the undesirable forms of commercial sponsorship discussed earlier.

We have found that the existence of this peg on which to hang British action in sports overseas is valuable. Our publication *Sports Exchange World** brings matters, once kept in the dark, right into the open. People overseas, tired of the protocol involved in reaching the many and various British sports associations directly, can send one letter to us and we handle the protocol while placing the matter in the hands of the most suitable expert. We have found that colleges and universities are able to work more freely than 'organisations' in this area; they can make immediate judgements on costings and placings. They must be at the forefront of such international action; they can elaborate the tailor-made courses which are essential to developing countries. There is intense competition from the Americans, the West and East Germans, the French and the Russians in international sports aid.

At the time of writing, forty-one Britons are involved in the direction of international sports federations. Those federations with headquarters in Britain** should, we feel, have generous state support towards their buildings and administration. Our steering committee represents the major organisations actually working in — and thinking about — these problems. We would like in addition the active involvement of the British Council, the Sports Council, the Ministry of Overseas Development and others. Sadly, no such collaboration seems to be forthcoming; indeed we have

*Journal of the Centre for International Sports Studies, edited by James Platt, Chairman of the CISS and Director of the Central Bureau of Educational Visits and Exchanges, 44 Baker Street, London W1.
**See Appendix A.

even had individual cases of what can only be called wasteful obstruction of effort. What a tragedy this administrative jealousy has become.

As an example of this I turn to a recent experience in the Sudan. Passing through Khartoum, I was asked by the resident British Council representative if I could propose *urgently* a course of study for the Sudan national tennis coach. This I did. It was my intention to work through the Centre for International Sports Studies of which I was the Director — a reasonable desire, I think. Having arranged for the required course and winning the support of the several bodies in education and tennis who were concerned, I found that my guns were being spiked by the joint action of persons in the London office of the British Council and in the Sports Council. I received a panic call from the tennis coach in the Sudan saying that he was literally 'waiting at the airport', but that he could not depart because the London end of the British Council had informed him that his course was not ready. It is embarrassing to have to try to explain such behaviour to overseas visitors — especially when, after needless delays, the visitor receives a course nearly identical to the original! I never received a full explanation; the nearest to it was a garbled description of a protocol arrangement in such matters agreed between the British Council and the Sports Council. 'Obstruction' is the most kindly word I can think of but there are stronger descriptions. We can well do without this sordid institutional rivalry.

In this area it is particularly important to get things right because the image of the country abroad is involved. Enough of the past; what we need now is agreement by all concerned to collaborate and work towards an agreed objective. The British voice must be heard loud and clear in all the corridors of international sport and physical education. One can hope that the secretariat of the Association of National Olympic Committees might take up residence in London; there has been collaboration between the Government, the Sports Council and the British Olympic Association in packaging a British bid to this end. A similar joint package between sport, and national government, and including local government, might result in a bid for the 1988 Olympic Games. The appropriate Olympic bodies — the Association of National Olympic Committees, and the International Olympic Committee — will decide on these matters. It is this sort of imaginative gesture in which national pride has a part that is badly needed if we are to have a future in the administration of sport.

I am left with two remaining matters of great importance — one *ideological*, one *financial*. The *ideological* factor is that of sport as work. The old dividing lines between amateur and professional are blurred. Hundreds of thousands of people worldwide earn their living by some association with sport. There are teachers of physical education. (Many sports, it should be said, have always made exceptions for professional teachers of physical education when it came to amateur legislation: 'full-time' teaching of sport was not allowed, but if the PE teacher took one lesson in another area this made the whole thing allowable. Sometimes there was not even this requirement.) There are those who work in the sports media, professional sportsmen and the razzamatazz of managers, public relations people and marketing associates who surround them. There is the whole field of sports centre management and sports tourism. The hobbies connected with sport have sparked off industries concerned with manufacture and marketing. There are competitions from the children's comic type to the national lottery. The manufacture and distribution of sports equipment and clothing is becoming a major world industry; witness the rise of the Adidas company. Sponsorship could perhaps become the *major* influence in sport in some countries.

At the top of this great pyramid are those who search for the ultimate excellence in sport: some choose to do it full-time and for financial gain, while others choose to prepare at the same time for a future professional life. The sports star can be compared with an artist. But sport is a transient art; we all age and nothing is more sad than the ageing sportsman with the Peter Pan complex. We all take great pleasure in watching supreme art in sport; we want those who represent us to be fully prepared; we want them also not to suffer economically for the sacrifices and the self-discipline by which they reach fulfilment. Sometimes we think absolute professionalism is the only answer — then along come Sebastian Coe and Malmö Football Club to remind us that there is a 'part-time' way also. The problem of 'amateurism' has been with us almost since the beginning of organised competitive sport. Certainly it was one of the motives behind the rejuvenation of the modern Olympic Games. The problem is different in countries where great geographical distances mean that the assembling of a national team calls for absence from work for several days or weeks. It is different in developing countries where only the state can initiate action. It is different in sports where mere children become world champions; in gymnastics we no longer worry about professionalism but whether children can complete normal schooling without psychological damage — perhaps even physical damage.

The 'lifestyle of the star', paid or unpaid, has become a major motivating force for sports success throughout the world. The search for success has led to experiments in skill, in training and in imagination, ranging from the bizarre and the accidental to the macabre and the fatal. The fact that this drive for success — in itself amoral — can be unaccompanied by a permanent educational programme (in the widest sense) has led us to the present situation where drug abuse in sport must be handled by 'testing procedures'. The fully educated sportsman, aware of the miraculous nature of the human organism, conscious of the symbolic and truly chivalrous nature of sport, would not dream of interfering with the delicate chemical balances of his body-mind — merely for the pursuit of sports success. Nor would an educated coach or an educated medical adviser. The 'educated' star would be supported by his community in return for his representing them well; there would be no talk of his being responsible only unto himself. There is no star yet who should not thank his family, his teachers, his clubs, his federation and all those who graciously act as cannon fodder. It is this *educational* problem which is a major ideological problem in the world of international sport. There is no easy answer. If there were, there would be no problem. Is there anything we can do in the meantime — except struggle on?

I propose that we all seriously study the possibility of *special symbolic open meetings*. They would be major events open to amateurs and professionals. They would be symbolic in that they would subscribe to the traditional ethics of 'amateur sport': that is, there would be no money prizes, no gambling, no obvious material rewards. Any revenue raised would be donated to good causes in the world of sport.

Some traditional events might be designated open and symbolic. Wimbledon is a case in point. I am sure that the money motive is secondary among Wimbledon participants. Without enormous prizes Wimbledon would continue. Sometimes I feel that the sudden withdrawal of massive financial involvement in sport might not be a bad thing. We would be back to grass roots, rethinking our reasons for sport, rebuilding again from first principles. Are such ideas beyond the wit of the International Olympic Committee, the professional entrepreneurs and the international federations? I know they are not; the International Table Tennis Federation recognises only 'players'; the 'Dubai Golden' events in international athletics are a partial recognition. *Open, symbolic events in which the emphasis is on fairplay and sport's intrinsic worth would be an exciting and inspiring development throughout sport.*

The *financial* problem is a major one. We can *all* dream up great ideas, but before they can be brought to fruition, the question of who is going to pay for them has to be faced. Personally I am in favour of collective responsibility for the provision of major services required for civilised living. I rate sport in the same category as health and education. I have no objection to being taxed for such advantages. I believe that the state, national and local, should budget heavily for sport, for reasons which I trust are made clear in this text. I believe we should go further than we have ever done in community subsidies for sports facilities, for sports coaching, for sports transportation at national competitive level.

I believe that sport would profit immensely from changes in laws relating to Purchase Tax and Value Added Tax, rate relief and charity status. I believe in a multi-sport structure in which the rich sports subsidise the poor. I believe in sponsorship by local government as well as by industry: such sponsorship and patronage should be regulated and made permanent and continuous, and it should be subject to certain ethical considerations — such as the pursuit of health.

Now, for the first time in Britain, three teams in three different sports, each playing in a national league and using the same community facilities, will be sponsored by a commercial company, Kelly Services, who have chosen to aid the teams with regard to clothing, travel (in the form of a motorised caravan sleeping fourteen people, a boon for away matches) and part-accommodation expenses. Representing respectively, basketball, table tennis and volleyball, the teams play at the Tolworth Recreation Centre in Surrey. They intend to play in European competition, and have changed their name to 'Kelly Girl Internationals'. This development indicates the move towards multi-sport organisation and collaborative sponsorship, on which many sports will have to rely in the near future. It involves a dual-use community facility on a school site. The intention is to give the operation a continuity of at least five years. The company's previous experience of sports sponsorship has been with motor racing and they found it rewarding; the publicity, they say, was greater than anything which could have been 'bought' commercially for a similar outlay.

I believe that stadia and centres should belong primarily to the people who utilise them and are spectators at them, and that more profits should go back into the clubs and the sports. Community ownership and management of sports facilities brings with it community responsibility. Is it possible that we can make sport so attractive to young people *en masse* that they will defend — *en masse* — that which clearly is theirs, and which makes their life so much more worthwhile? Vandalism of community-owned facilities could become no more than a bad memory. I believe in self-help schemes, in physical labour on site, in fund-raising, so that solidarity becomes an actual experience. Sport should respond flexibly to developing social and environmental phenomena; the current energy crisis alone should stimulate us to work on more *tournaments* which involve several teams, and fewer matches involving only two; the idea of multi-sport festivals should receive a boost for the same reason.

I feel that the buying and selling of football players for astronomical and ever-soaring prices is a disgrace to a society where the provision of play and sport areas and programmes in urban centres is deplorable at best, and non-existent at worst. Would not a tax on these massive football player transfers be legitimate: a special tax on every transfer, for the direct benefit of the general sports fund?

There are growing rumours — with some substance, it seems — of large payments to 'amateur' athletes; the sooner such irregularities are cleared up, the sooner can the sport in general benefit fairly from such payments — if in fact they are made. I have already pointed out in this book that some countries, in tennis, have had to handle this problem — some insist on all monies going to the national federation and a proportion being made over to the athlete concerned; some arrange an equitable distribution between player and federation; some have no law which covers the situation, but 'encourage' the player to take part in high-level exhibition matches in aid of the national federation.

I believe that the media should pay heavily for sport. The help which a Japanese television company gave to the national Japanese volleyball squads is a good model. In return for guaranteed first division volleyball on Sunday evenings, this company financed long tours for the Japanese men and women teams in Europe and the Americas; this is the major reason why Japan has managed to stay at the forefront of world volleyball despite a geographical isolation from the main volleyball competitive centres. Allied to this is the generous help which Japanese industry gives to sport in terms of employment opportunities for talented sports people.

Finally, I believe that the secret for a financial revolution in sport stares us in the face week after week. *Sport should, in some way, 'take over' the national football pools.* If this is unthinkable to a majority, then sport should launch its own national lottery to compete fiercely with those that have cheerfully bled the sports movement for so many years. Isn't it clear that even a mere change in the distribution of the 'dividends' — with no attack on profits — would transform British sport? This alone would create facilities and fund coaching schemes, and provide building and maintenance work. It is the massive greed which makes such a simple strategy for prize distribution impossible to consider which I cannot understand. I have the feeling that if the Sports Council were to devote itself entirely, for one year, to this major problem, it would do immense good.

Lastly I want to mention great people in sport. I make a plea for the eccentric, the unorthodox. I make a plea that their opinions, whoever they are, be always considered by the sporting establishment. In writing this book, I have no single model of sporting organisation in mind. I resist the idea that there can be one grey norm to which we will all have to conform. The panorama of world sport is for ever shifting; it calls for constant innovation and adaptability. If I had to make a choice, I would invest in people rather than facilities. A high teacher-to-taught ratio is always preferable to palaces of sport devoid of coaches. I recognise the contribution to world sport made by Britons like Philip Noel-Baker and Stanley Rous, ninety and eighty years old respectively — grand old men of sport who still, despite their age, still have an intimate intellectual involvement with the sports movement. I believe in youth and the need to involve them much more at all levels of sport; but I do not believe that sport should be abandoned completely to them. Sport still provides a significant bridge between generations.

In 1979 the first British honorary degree for service to sport was awarded by Loughborough University to Lord Noel-Baker, whose life makes him the ideal Olympian. Silver medallist in the Olympic 1500 metres in 1920; commandant of the British team in Helsinki in 1952; President of Unesco's International Council of Sport and Physical Education; late Professor of International Relations in the University of London; founder of the Friends Ambulance Units; one time Secretary of State for the Commonwealth; Nobel Peace Prize winner of 1959. If there is any one person to whom I wish to pay tribute in this book it is Philip Noel-Baker — a wise friend and a wonderful 'Friend'. And in saying this I recall a memorable statement of his: 'After a lifetime in world affairs, I have found sport to be the most rich, the most noble. In a nuclear age, sport is man's best hope.'

This book is meant to stimulate people to think more about the basic role of sport and physical education in society. I have tried to work on the principle that 'facts plus discussion' is better than 'facts plus propaganda'. I hope I have set people thinking divergently as well as convergently. I hope my own pedigree in sport will help people to accept my criticisms. I have spent a lifetime in sport; I train teachers of physical education; I coach, and I lecture and write about sport. I love sport. This is not a book about sports philosophy or even about sports administration. It is about a sports strategy. A strategy is about decisions — today, tomorrow, in the future. A strategy cannot wait for a fully thought-out ideology. It must be pragmatic — and it must allow for the many viewpoints and opinions that seek recognition. I also believe that sport is most suitable for 'open government'. My plea to the new generation is: sport belongs to everyone — *to you*; don't abandon it.

Apppendix A

INTERNATIONAL SPORTS ORGANISATIONS WITH HEADQUARTERS IN THE UNITED KINGDOM

International Amateur Athletics Federation
International Equestrian Federation
International Yacht Racing Federation
International Federation of Association Football
International Rugby Football Board
International Cricket Conference
International Lawn Tennis Federation
International Table Tennis Federation
International Badminton Federation
International Archery Federation
International Tug of War Federation
International Federation of Ten Pin Bowling
International Power Lifting Federation
International Council of Sport and Physical Education
International Physical Education Federation
International Sports Medicine Federation
Secretariat, Commonwealth Games Federation

Appendix B

UNITED KINGDOM MEMBERS OF INTERNATIONAL SPORTS ORGANISATIONS*

H.R.H. Prince Philip	President, International Equestrian Federation
John Andrews	General Secretary, International Physical Education Federation
Jack Bailey	General Secretary, International Cricket Conference
Sir Roger Bannister	President, International Council of Sport and Physical Education
Pat Besford	Secretary, International Association of Sports Press (European Section)
Tony Brooks	General Secretary, International Tennis Federation
John Coghlan	General Secretary, International Council of Sport and Physical Education
K.S. Duncan	Secretary, Commonwealth Games Federation
Roy Evans	President, International Table Tennis Federation
Marquis of Exeter	Member, International Olympic Committee
Sir Denis Follows	Member, Executive Committee, Permanent Assembly of National Olympic Committee
Inga Frith	Life President, International Archery Federation
Maurice Glazer	President, International Federation of Ten Pin Bowling
Arthur Gold	President, European Amateur Athletics Association
David Gray	General Secretary, International Lawn Tennis Federation
Nigel Hacking	General Secretary, International Yacht Racing Federation
George Hilton	President, International Tug of War Federation
John Holt	General Secretary, International Amateur Athletics Federation
William Jones	Founder/Life General Secretary, International Amateur Basketball Federation (a U.K. citizen domiciled in Munich)

*At the time of going to press.

John Kane	Vice President, International Council of Health, Physical Education and Recreation
Lord Luke of Pavenham	Member, International Olympic Committee
David McNair	Vice President, History of International Sport and Physical Education Association
Vic Mercer	Chairman, International Power Lifting Federation
Keith Mitchell	Executive Member, International Amateur Basketball Federation
Ivor Montague	Founder-President, International Table Tennis Federation
Lord Noel-Baker	Life President, International Council of Sport and Physical Education
Raymond Owen	President, International Association of Olympic Medical Officers
Charles Palmer	President, World Judo Federation; General Secretary, General Assembly of International Sports Federation
Sir Alexander Ross	President, Commonwealth Games Federation
Sir Stanley Rous	Life President, International Federation of Association Football
V. Rowan	General Secretary, International Badminton Federation
Norman Sarsfield	Honorary Secretary, European Swimming Federation
Alec Smith	General Secretary, International Association of Olympic Medical Officers
Oscar State	Secretary, Commonwealth Weightlifting Federation
Frank Taylor	President, European Section, International Association of Sports Press
D. Thompson	General Secretary, International Archery Federation
Arthur Vint	Honorary General Secretary, International Table Tennis Federation
Allen Wade	Technical Committee, European Association Football Association
Bob Wight	Executive Member, International University Sport Federation (Physical Education Committee)
John Williams	General Secretary, International Sports Medical Federation
Sir Walter Winterbottom	Chairman Sports Development Committee (Council of Europe)

INDEX